The Savvy Supervisor
Helping Employees Manage Themselves

William C. Willging, Ph.D.

ISBN: 0692640754
ISBN-13: 978-0692640753

DEDICATION

This book is dedicated to the memory of my parents, Jim and
Audrey Willging. Talk about *luck…*

CONTENTS

ACKNOWLEDGMENTS

First and forever I want to thank the one who knows me the best, and *still* agreed to marry me—Patricia. She's in front of, beside, and behind me always in whatever I do. If there weren't a Patricia, there wouldn't be a book. I love you, P2.

Next, I owe an immeasurable debt of gratitude to a long-time friend and colleague, Jeff Glindmeyer. He's the founder of the "Writers Club"—our two-person, mutual-support, book-writing group. Without his advice and encouragement I would still be stuck at the "I should write a book" stage. Thank you, Jeff, for your enduring friendship and your unflagging support.

I also want to thank Ross Pollard who is my financial advisor, friend, and now book reviewer. His feedback was extremely valuable, as is everything he does for me.

Many thanks to Dave Person—a great neighbor and outstanding copy editor—for making sure I dotted my t's and crossed my i's.

Finally, there are the thousands of managers and supervisors who participated in my training programs over all these years. Their feedback and suggestions honed the content of this book. Their continued endorsement of the program ensured its validity, integrity and relevance. They kept it real.

.

INTRODUCTION

A recent search for "supervisory skills" on the website of a popular online book retailer returned over 3,000 titles. Clearly this is a popular topic! And just as clearly, there's no shortage of ideas about how to supervise people.

So Why This Book?

"The Savvy Supervisor" is the written version of a training program I've been conducting for over 20 years in all types of organizations—public, private, for-profit and non-profit. This program consistently receives highly positive reviews from the supervisors who participate in the program as well as from their managers who send them to the training—mostly because:

- The concepts are simply presented and easily understood.

- The concepts are easily applied by anyone attempting them.

- Those who use the concepts get very good results—not just in the productivity of the employees they supervise, but also in employee attitudes and motivation.

Who Is This Book For?

This book is intended for *any* supervisor, whether you just started or you've been managing people for years. I've had many participants who have been supervising for upwards of 20 years tell me how much they learned from my program, and what good results they were getting by applying the concepts.

So no matter how extensive your supervisory experience is, this book will show you how to continuously improve your ability to successfully guide the work of others.

What you'll learn here is that supervising people is really just common sense—but not always common practice.

The Scope of This Book

I want to briefly explain what I'll be covering in this book.

One size doesn't fit all. Supervision is a big topic with a lot of facets to it and ways to think about it. No single source can cover the whole topic in one fell swoop (...well, maybe it *could* but you'd need a small library to hold it all!)

This book is focused on the *basics* of effective employee supervision. It covers what it means to be a supervisor and how to do that role well. It presents a *daily* approach for constantly developing employees to be as competent as they can be, communicating with them, and helping them be as "self-managing" as possible.

I'll be explaining how the traditional supervisory practices that have been in use for literally centuries are no longer effective. I'll be presenting an alternative approach that breaks with traditional practices and results not only in employees producing high quality work, but also in greatly enhanced employee initiative, job-ownership, and morale.

When you've mastered this alternative approach, you've mastered supervision in any organization, at any level, at any time.

Written Procedures

Managing people effectively is the focus of this book. However, there's one aspect of managing people I won't cover. I won't tell you how to follow the various formal HR policies and procedures that most organizations have—conducting performance reviews, interviewing job applicants, corrective action plans, setting compensation levels, etc. Why?

Well, formal policies and procedures vary widely from organization to organization. So I can't describe a single approach for doing them all because there isn't a single approach that fits them all.

However, I'll still offer you some big help here. If you follow the daily, minute-by-minute practices of effective supervision I'll be showing you, it will be much easier for you to follow your organization's HR policies and procedures, no matter what they are.

You'll have a detailed knowledge of job requirements and employees' ability to meet those requirements, based on your daily interactions and observations of their work. Armed with that knowledge you'll be able to do a great job of following whatever HR procedures your organization has in place, and filling out whatever forms they call for.

Four Fundamental Topics

This book is organized into four topics that I consider *fundamental* to supervising people well:

Part 1: *THE ROLE OF THE SUPERVISOR*—what the job is really all about.

To be an effective supervisor, you have to first understand what it *means* to be a supervisor. What is your role? What are your responsibilities as far as managing employees? What authority do you have—and *not* have? What is the nature of the supervisor-employee relationship?

Part 2: *COACHING VS. BOSSING*— how to best do that job.

You have to understand the best ways to carry out the supervisor's role. There are various approaches to daily supervision, some very effective, some not. What are the differences, which are better, and why?

Part 3: *COMMUNICATING EFFECTIVELY*—how to talk to them, how to listen to them.

You can't supervise employees if you aren't able to truly communicate with them. That not only means communicating clearly *to* them, but equally important, being able to really *listen* to them.

Part 4: *THE PROBLEM PERFORMER*—what's gone wrong and how to fix it.

On occasion you may find yourself faced with supervising a problem performer—one who fairly consistently fails to produce the work results you're asking for. It's very important to know how to deal with that employee effectively. You have to have a good way to figure out what the employee's problem is and how to get it resolved efficiently and effectively.

I'll go through those four parts in order, building on the basic concepts as I go. There's something in here for every supervisor, whether you're brand-new or an "old hand" at it!

Let's get to it!

PART 1

THE ROLE OF THE SUPERVISOR

The supervisor's role is one of the most, if not *the* most, important roles in any organization. Supervisors are the intermediaries between organizational goals and implementation. They make sure people successfully do the organization's work to produce the organization's products, services, etc. The organization's survival absolutely depends on supervisors doing their jobs well.

I've heard it said that people join *organizations*, but they leave *supervisors*. Think about that for a second. People agree to go to work for an organization, but it's the supervisor's actions that determine whether or not employees decide to stay in the organization. If supervisors don't do their jobs effectively, employees don't stay. Organizations don't thrive if employees are bailing out over the way supervisors manage them.

In Part 1, I'll talk to you about:

- What it really means to be a supervisor.
- Being a *leader*—because that's really what a supervisor is.
- How just about anybody can be a leader.
- The way most people typically get promoted to supervisor.
- The changes that happen in supervisors' day-to-day work as a result of being promoted.
- Three very important mindsets I strongly believe supervisors need to adopt about themselves and the employees reporting to them in order to be really effective.

Part 1 will identify what it really *means* to be a supervisor. That sets the stage for the rest of the book which addresses how to actually *do* what effective supervisors do.

1 LEADERSHIP

Effective supervisors are not just good managers—they are also good *leaders*.

They don't just manage what has to get done, by when, and within what quality standards. They also lead and inspire employees to do their best, and help them continuously learn to manage their own work.

They expect employees to make decisions, solve problems, improve processes, and in general be constantly *thinking* about what they are doing at any and every point of their workday.

In this book, when I use the term "supervisor," I am referring to someone who is not only a manager, but also a leader.

Born or Made?

As a supervisor you are expected to be a good leader. There is a long-standing debate of sorts about whether leaders are born or made. It's an interesting question if you are a philosopher, but isn't very helpful if you are, or are about to become, a supervisor.

You're born who you are, and that's what you've got to work with. But don't worry—you're going to be just fine, and here's why. Just about anybody can learn to be a good supervisor—and a good leader—by simply following some basic concepts that really are just common sense.

One way to look at "Leadership"

Leadership has been studied every which way to Sunday over the decades. A common approach has been to identify people thought to be excellent leaders and then "dissect" their personalities to see what makes them tick.

Countless books, articles and papers describe various characteristics of excellent leaders based on personality types and strengths, ways of thinking, personal habits, ethics, whether they comply with rules or not, their motivations, values, etc.

The gist of what these approaches are saying is that leadership is a function of who these leaders *ARE*. And so the thinking goes, all you need to do is be just like them —imitate the personalities and personal habits of these excellent leaders—and, *voila!*, you'll be a leader too!

However....

You *aren't* just like them. (Truth be told, they aren't just like each other, either!) You are uniquely you. You have your own personality, your own strengths, beliefs and values.

If good leadership means you have to be just like somebody else then you're probably sunk. You can't really change who you are to be just like them. You may *try* to be like them, but you'll only be able to do that at the cost of not being yourself, not being who you really are. Good luck with that.

Nope, you're stuck with being who you are—but that's *great*! The truth is, you can be an excellent leader by just being yourself—no trade-offs required.

> *The truth is, you can be an excellent leader by just being yourself—no trade-offs required.*

So What Is "Leadership" Then?

Good news! Leadership is basically how you *act*, not who you *are*. It's what you say and how you say it, how you react to employee ideas and inputs, handle their mistakes, recognize their successes, help them develop, teach them new skills. Your external actions with employees make or break you as a leader.

Two people who have nearly identical personalities can be as different as night and day in how well they lead. By the same token, two people with completely different personalities can lead equally well.

You can be born with all the personality credentials research has to offer, but if you don't act right you're not going to lead well as a supervisor.

I'll show you how to be an excellent supervisor by *acting* like one while still *being* exactly who you are. I'll show you the *behaviors* of effective supervision.

2 THE ROAD TO GLORY

What Happened?

How did you get to be a supervisor? What's changed? What do you personally produce now? What kind of authority do you have? How should you think about your role?

I'm willing to bet you were made a supervisor before you'd ever really thought about those questions in any depth. I'll also bet no one sat you down and really explained the role to you, at least as far as the people management side of the job. Turns out this wouldn't be at all unusual. Happens all the time. So, how did it happen to you?

In the Beginning

If you're like most of us your first job wasn't the kind of thing you saw yourself doing for thirty or forty years. It probably didn't pay a king's ransom, and wasn't all that personally fulfilling either.

I got my first real job, for example, when I was 8 years old. I worked one summer for a local bakery—*"Spudnuts"*—riding my bike through my neighborhood trying to sell donuts door-to-door. By mid-morning on a hot summer day, my supply of still-not-sold donuts—which was always the bulk of them—mostly just attracted a customer base of several hundred flies.

Fortunately for me, every morning after I'd spent a few hours riding around trying to sell my donuts, my mother would bail me out by buying up what remained in my basket—a gooey mass of melted, fly-infested dough and icing that thankfully she didn't make me eat!

As I said—no king's ransom there, and certainly no real future!

Like me, after a first little job, you likely had a series of jobs until eventually you got to a full-time job that paid well enough to stick with, that you didn't mind—maybe even *enjoyed*—doing. Over time, it became apparent you had a knack for the work. You got better and better at it and began to get a reputation for being a hotshot at it. Coworkers came to you for help, and your bosses relied on *you* when they really needed to get it done right. The money kept getting better, and so did the recognition by management. Seemed like this job thing was working out pretty well!

Then one day it happened.

Management came to you all smiles. They heaped on the praise. They talked about how appreciated you were. They bragged up the great work you were doing. They said they wished they had an *army* of people like you working for them.

Then they said they had a deal for you...

Let's Make A Deal

They were promoting you to supervisor! You'd been chosen (probably from among those you'd been working side-by-side with) to take the reins and be in charge. You had arrived! You'd get more money, higher status, greater recognition from upper management, etc.

You might have been a bit giddy at first, kind of like the time an actress won an Oscar and during

*And then it hit you like a ton of bricks—WHAT had you just gotten yourself into? You didn't know how to **supervise**!*

her acceptance speech looked tearfully out over the audience and said, "You really DO like me, don't you!!" You were filled with pride, gratitude, and excitement. Your hard work had finally paid off and you were being rewarded BIG TIME! Oh yeah! Life was good!

And then it hit you like a ton of bricks—WHAT had you just gotten yourself into? You didn't know how to *supervise*! Your former friends and coworkers looked at you like you had suddenly grown an extra hand out of your forehead. Great waves of skepticism and distrust were rolling in all around you.

Older workers scoffed. They said things like you were "Wet behind the ears!" Or, they called you a "Whipper-snapper!"

Younger workers rolled their eyes. "Dinosaur!" "Out of touch!" they said.

Your friends might have begun to treat you like you were the enemy ("Brown-noser!" "Hypocrite!"). Forget the Wednesday after-work beers with your buddies, and kiss the weekend barbecues with them goodbye, too.

You weren't sure what management expected of you, and you were now *way* too visible to them to be seen as being unsure of yourself.

You had to talk to managers you'd never talked to before, about things you'd never even thought about. Nowhere to hide.

A plague of things now became your responsibility...things somebody else (read that "your boss") used to do. Paperwork, meetings, reports, explanations, directions, plans, schedules, assignments.

Would you succeed or would you come crashing down in a glorious, blazing ball of incompetence? Would you still be employed if this didn't work out? Were you now lawsuit bait for every disgruntled employee who took issue with something you said or did? Did you now have to show you were as good as, or better than, the employees you supervise at doing their jobs? Would you have to endure hazing, resistance, arguments, ridicule?

Wow, that's a lot to think about all of a sudden. But wait—there's *more*!

Don't Do That—Do This

Here's perhaps the weirdest part of this promotion deal. In a fairly perverse turn of events, the very thing that got you promoted in the first place is what you were now being asked to stop doing—the actual work itself. Others would do that work.

In a fairly perverse turn of events, the very thing that got you promoted in the first place is what you were now being asked to stop doing...

In its place, you'd now be doing something else. And what was that? How about something you had little-to-no clue how to do—manage people!

What??? Make a star performer stop doing the very thing they're so good at, and instead make them do something they basically don't have a clue how to do? Does that make *any* sense at all?

Well, it may seem completely illogical on the face of it, but this is exactly how most promotions happen in most organizations most of the time. Organizations tend to take their best technical performers and turn them into supervisors. It's been the typical pattern for a very long time.

There aren't any villains, here. It's just a very old practice that's based on the faulty assumption that if *you* know how to do the work well, then certainly you can get *others* to do the work well.

If You Can Sing, Surely You Can Ride a Bike!

The fact of the matter is that doing work well and managing people well are two *very* different, almost completely unrelated skills. Just because you can do the work well doesn't mean you automatically can manage people well, too. We all know superstars who excel at doing the work, but have the personality and people skills of a rattlesnake. And we also know people who are truly gifted at managing others, but couldn't do the work if their lives depended on it. The two skills simply do not tend to fit naturally together like hand and glove for very many supervisors.

So if this quirky turn of events left you feeling lost and panicky, that's really okay. It's *normal*. In fact it would be far more worrisome if you *didn't* feel a bit—if not a *lot*—puckered up! The concerns you had showed you were actually paying attention and thinking about exactly the right things.

It wasn't about you. It was about the situation. You'd been promoted to a job you'd had no training for. Who wouldn't feel concerned and anxious? But fortunately supervising well is something almost anyone can learn.

Supervising people well is a matter of first knowing what you need to do and then doing it consistently. All that's required to learn it is a desire to be really good at it. You bring that desire, and I'll give you the insights and how-to's for doing it well.

Learning the Ropes

The first step to being an excellent supervisor is to understand what it really *means* to be a supervisor. If you're like most, you've likely picked up some faulty perceptions about the role through the course of your work life. It's basically how you've most likely been trained to view the role.

Trained you say? Yup. *What training?*

Oh, you may not have taken any courses or seminars about how to supervise, but rest assured you've been trained. By whom? All the supervisors and managers whom you've been exposed to throughout your work life. They've trained you informally by the example they've set.

You've observed them directly and indirectly over time, watched how they did their thing, and tried to imitate them. You learned how to act and think like them.

And they, in turn, learned how to supervise in exactly the same way—they imitated those who went before them, who learned from those who went before *them*, and so on. It's basically passive, accidental training that happens subtly and informally for the most part. And therein lies the rub.

Will The Circle Be Unbroken?

Since most supervisors have had little-to-no formal training, they have just continued on supervising the way it's always been done. The thinking and the methods—both good and bad—have continued pretty much unchallenged and unchanged for a couple hundred years.

A quick thought for you. How many critical processes in your organization have gone basically unchanged for a couple hundred years? Think about work procedures, accounting methods, technologies, inventory management, logistics.

And yet here's one of the most critical processes in any organization—managing the people who do the work—that's continued on for about that long, basically unchanged, unimproved. Seems a little weird, doesn't it? But that's how it's been.

Now that all by itself would not be such a bad thing—*if* this traditional way to supervise was the best way. It turns out, however, that this approach to supervision is actually at the core of most of the people-management problems supervisors face every day. It creates most of the problems supervisors have in motivating employees and ensuring they produce high quality job results.

I'll talk about a better way in Part 2 of this book—*Bossing vs. Coaching.*

It's All In Your Mind!

I'm going to start by talking to you about three key perspectives ("mindsets") that *all* supervisors need to have embedded in their heads if they have any hope of being really effective. These

21

mindsets are critical for success, regardless of any specific style of supervising.

These three perspectives define what the role of a supervisor *really* is—what it truly means to be a supervisor. Operating out of any other way of looking at the role of a supervisor is a prescription for disaster.

3 CHANGING YOUR MIND

The first step in understanding the supervisor's role is looking at how to *think* about it. Your views and beliefs (your "mindsets") about the supervisor's role dictate every little detail and nuance of how you supervise day-to-day.

> *The first step in understanding the supervisor's role is looking at how to **think** about it.*

How you think about the supervisor role and employees is absolutely critical in determining whether you will be a really effective supervisor or not. So I'm going to work on your mind first before talking about the mechanics of supervising.

Everything in this book flows from three key mindsets.

Mindset One: Your Product

The first mindset is knowing what your primary product is now that you're a supervisor.

Before you were promoted to supervisor, your direct product was some sort of work result—something you produced for the good of the cause. It was either something tangible or a service of some sort. Once you became a supervisor it was no longer your job to produce that product or service yourself.

So if that's no longer your product, what's replaced it in your new role? What do you produce now? Well, when you were put in charge of managing people, your product became *competent people.*

You're still held responsible for the quality of the work the employees you supervise produce. But now you ensure quality work results by making sure the people you supervise can, and do, produce them. If those people are competent and motivated, quality product happens.

If there's a problem with the results the people you supervise are producing, your job is to find out if they have a competency problem and fix it. Notice I am saying you fix the *competency problem*, not the product itself. The work results get fixed by you improving the employee's competency.

Here I Come To Save The Day!!

It's a *huge* challenge for most supervisors to avoid the temptation to dive in and do the work themselves when something goes awry. Why? Well, remember the good old days when you excelled at that work—before you got promoted? Remember how that was the way you built your reputation, and it was what gave you

For any of you who are of the "if you want it done right you gotta do it yourself" school of thought, you have to get over that malarkey right now.

such satisfaction? Remember how good it felt to know what you were doing and how confident you felt doing it?

Well, when something heads south with the work, the big temptation is for you to get sucked right back into that former comfort zone. When you're faced with a choice of either doing something you're not so confident about—managing the people—or doing something you're very confident about—doing the work itself—the urge to jump in and do the work yourself can be almost irresistible. Especially if your management is hot on your trail to get things fixed and back on track ASAP.

For any of you who are of the *"if you want it done right you gotta do it yourself"* school of thought, you have to get over that malarkey right now. It just isn't your job anymore. If you want it done right, make sure the *employees* are competent enough to do it right.

More to the point, you CAN'T do it all yourself. At times you may have to do *some* of the work yourself (if you're a team lead you may be *required* to). But not all of it. There's just too much of it. That's why all those other people have been hired to do it.

If you want the work done right, then it's your job to make sure the people whose job it is know how to do it right and can do it.

The Silver Lining

There's a real benefit for you in all this by the way. Contrary to what many think, you don't actually *have* to be able to do their jobs to supervise them because it isn't *your* job to do that work. It's theirs. You just have to be able to tell if they're producing the results you're asking for.

You aren't in competition with them, and you don't have to "prove" to them you can do their work. That's not *your* job. It's *theirs*.

So, mindset number one—competent people are your product. Work results are their product. You personally impact the quality of work results by focusing your attention on managing people in ways that develop and maintain their competence.

Mindset Two: The Authority You Have

Authority comes with the job for sure. But what *kind* of authority?

Are the employees you supervise your direct descendants? No? Then you aren't their parent.

Do you monitor their behavior all day and whenever they break a rule write them a ticket and send them off to court? No? Then you aren't a cop.

Have they done something very wrong and been forced to work for you for five years to life? No? Then you aren't a warden.

Are you supposed to watch over them all day and make sure they are fed, kept warm, entertained and getting at least one nap per day? No? Then you aren't a babysitter.

There's a New Sheriff in Town

One of the most prevalent misconceptions in the informal training I earlier said you had gotten is the idea that those are the sorts of authority supervisors have. That in some sense they "own" the employees reporting to them. That they are smarter, better, more mature than the people reporting to them. That they get to lord it over them. That they are the grand puppet masters who get to make people do whatever they want to.

I've heard supervisors refer to employees as idiots, babies, brats. I've heard them call employees petty, immature, whiny, irresponsible, contrary, disobedient, lazy. I've heard them accuse employees of having no work ethic, no ownership, no common sense, and big attitude problems.

And these supervisors are among the first to complain about unmotivated employees and poor work quality. There are a couple of big dots there—can you connect them?

If you want quality results from employees, you have to believe they can, and will, produce them.

You don't own the employees, they aren't your private army to order around as you see fit. They aren't your kids. They aren't your prisoners. You aren't a better, more worthwhile, higher-order human being than they are.

You'll notice that throughout this book I never use the words "*your employees,*" the people working "*under you,*" your "*subordinates,*" or infer that employees are inferior in any way to you or anyone else in management.

They are adults just as you are, and you need to acknowledge that and treat them accordingly. If you want quality results from employees, you have to believe they can, and will, produce them. If you want their respect you have to first give *them* respect. If you want them to act like adults you have to regard them, and treat them, as adults.

As You Sow, So Shall You Reap

The truth of the matter is they'll react to you according to how you treat them. If you treat them like you're their parent, they'll act like your kids. If you treat them like you're a warden, they'll act like prisoners. If you constantly look to catch them doing something wrong, they probably will.

Not sure how you're coming across to them? It's easy to tell. Look at how they're acting. If they're acting like responsible, intelligent motivated adults, then that's how you're treating them. If they act in any other way, then you're treating them in some other way. They react according to how you treat them. You literally get what you ask for. Think about that for a moment.

So, if you aren't a parent, warden, babysitter, etc., then what ARE you? You're a *facilitator*.

Back To the Authority Thing

Now that may seem like I'm playing some sort of word game with you, but "facilitator" literally describes your role as a supervisor. If your product is competent people, then it's your job to facilitate—*help*—them to be competent. You're responsible for making it as easy as possible for them to be successful—*competent.*

You do have clear authority as a supervisor. You have the authority to:

1. Define the work (you decide what needs to get done by when).

2. Assign the work (you decide who is to do what work, *you* define what their job is--a very important concept if they ever try to tell you something isn't their job!).

3. Allocate resources (it's your responsibility to make sure resources are available to those who need them to get their work done).

4. Enforce your organization's policies (you and the employees have to behave in accordance with your employer's written policies and procedures.

If you are unsure about the amount and/or nature of the authority you have in any of those four areas, put this book down and go to your manager ASAP and find out. If you don't know what your authority is, the people reporting to you certainly don't. And if they don't know, they'll tend to fill in the blanks themselves. They'll decide what authority they think you do and don't have. And generally that will be something more in line with their desires—not yours!

"I'm from Supervision and I'm Here to Help!"

There's huge benefit to you in all this facilitator stuff. Rather than make their day miserable, your job is basically to help them have a great day! All those fears you had at promotion time about how they would react to you if *...you do not have the authority to lord it over employees and rule by intimidation.* you were younger or older than them, or if they used to be your coworkers, just went *poof*! How could they resent anybody who is there to make sure they are as successful as possible?

Does it matter if you're older than they are? No, you're going to help them be successful.

Does it matter if you are younger than they are? No, you recognize how skilled they are and you're glad to have them on board. You're going to make it possible for them to use all that expertise and be successful.

Does it matter if they used to be your coworkers? No, you aren't there to order them around and act like you're better than they are. You're there to help them be successful.

So, mindset number two—you do not have the authority to lord it over employees and rule by intimidation. Instead, you have the authority to define the work, to allocate that work and the resources to do it to individual employees, and to enforce company policy. You have the authority to facilitate their success.

Mindset Three: The Contract

It may not be specifically written down anywhere in your organization, but there's a contract in effect between every employer and employee. It's a fairly simple contract. It goes like this:

Employer: "I have some work I want done and I agree to give you money and certain 'perks' for doing that work." Employee: "I agree to do that work."

As long as the employee does the work, the employer agrees to pay wages and extend perks. As long as the employer is paying the wages and extending the perks, the employee agrees to do the work. Simple, but *very* powerful.

As a supervisor you represent the Employer (the organization), and this contract powers everything you do in that role. It gives you the responsibility and the right to tell employees what work they need to accomplish. It authorizes you to compare what you've asked them to produce with what they actually do, or don't, produce. It's the bedrock of being a supervisor and the source of your formal authority.

Nothing Personal...

This contract also means that the relationship between the supervisor and employee is strictly business—not personal. That takes a lot of the emotion and heartburn out of supervising. It has nothing to do with who the employee is, and everything to do with the work. (You'll really see this benefit later on in this book when I discuss how to approach a problem performer.)

It is not about people, it's about *work*. It is not about how you or they feel about each other. It's unemotional. It's about whether a *business arrangement*—the "contract"—is being honored by both parties.

A Matter of Choice

This contract is voluntary for both parties. Either party can get out of the contract at any time, for any reason. (This is the basis of "at will" employment. The only exceptions to this arrangement are terminations conducted for reasons that are legally prohibited, such as race, age, ethnicity, certain disabilities, etc.)

That means as long as they choose to do the work, they are choosing to continue being a "member" of the organization. It also means that if they choose not to do that work, then they are essentially choosing to leave the organization. You may have to point out to them that this is a choice *they're* making, not you, but in fact that is what they're doing.

Notice how freeing this can be for *you*...all you are doing is enforcing the contract. If they do what they've agreed to do, they stay. If they don't, they have to go. Their choice. Their decision. Not yours.

Isn't That Obvious?

Well, you would think so—until you hear employees tell their supervisor, "That's not my job." Or, "You don't pay me enough to do that." Or you hear supervisors complain that they "can't get employees to do their jobs."

When employees act as if they're the ones who decide what their jobs are, or that they've got the option to do, or not do, what they're being asked to do, it's real clear they don't understand the contract.

You define what their job is, not them. The supervisor has the authority, and more importantly the *responsibility*, to define work results to employees and expect those results to be produced. Employees have the responsibility to produce those work results. Supervisors define work results, employees produce them.

Be Fair Now

Of course supervisors have to be correct when they decide what work needs to be done, and they have to be fair in assigning that work to the employees. And they have to be sure they're asking employees to do what the organization needs and not something the supervisor wants done for personal gain, or any other reason not directly related to work results. All work has to tie back to some organizational need or it isn't legitimate to ask any employee to do it.

So the concept of this contract is an extremely important concept. It will come up again and again in this book as I talk about ways to supervise effectively. It's key that you, and those you supervise, always keep this concept in the forefront of your brains.

Now that you understand these three key mindsets of the supervisor's role—what the *role* is, what kind of *authority* you do and don't have, and the *contract* —let's talk about is how to put them to use. I'm going to explain two contrasting styles for how to supervise—Bossing and Coaching.

PART 2

BOSSING
VS.
COACHING

An important clarification is in order. Although we often refer to a supervisor as a "boss," I am referring to a Boss in this book (capital "B") as a supervisor who uses the Bossing approach to supervising as opposed to one who uses the Coaching approach.

The two styles of supervising, Bossing and Coaching, are pretty much at the opposite ends of a spectrum. All supervisors tend to lean more toward one end of that spectrum than the other—some further than others.

In Part 2, I'm going to describe the two styles, and I'm going to give you some pretty compelling reasons why I think Coaching is the way to go.

Bossing is a very common supervisory style. Although it can be effective in getting work done, it comes with some pretty heavy costs to supervisors and to employees. I'll explain the "baggage" that comes with the Bossing style.

Coaching also can be effective in getting work done, producing as good (and usually better) work results as Bossing can. But it does so with far less negative fallout and personal frustration for everybody.

It empowers employees to manage their own work. It also generally results in much greater self confidence for you and for employees, deeper employee engagement, and higher employee morale.

4 THE TWO IT TAKES TO TANGO

We all need to know two things to accomplish anything successfully—we have to know WHAT we want to accomplish, and we have to know HOW to accomplish it. We usually fail when we don't have a clear idea of what we want to end up with. We also fail when we know *exactly* what we want to end up with but don't have a clue how do get there.

Simple concept? You betcha. But understanding how to apply that simple concept is essential to supervising effectively.

Put in really simple terms, people have to know the WHATs and the HOWs of their jobs to produce good work results—they have to know *what* results they're expected to produce, and they have to know *how* to produce them. If either of those two things is missing, or unclear, good work results won't happen.

You'll recall that your role as a supervisor is to make sure the people you supervise are *competent*. That means you have to make sure they clearly know what results you expect them to produce, and they're able to produce them.

The basic difference between Bosses and Coaches is how they manage the WHATs and HOWs of employees' jobs. Bosses and

Coaches do it in some profoundly different ways. As a result, they often get very different work results from those they supervise. They also tend to get very different motivation levels and attitudes from employees.

What About the WHAT?

According to the contract I described earlier between the employee and the organization, the employee agrees to produce the things the organization asks them to produce. Those things are work results, and employees have to know exactly WHAT those results are supposed to be if there's any hope they'll produce them.

That means knowing not only what constitutes a good result, but also when it has to be done (schedules) and where it goes when it's finished (delivery points, inventory locations, etc.).

Every task, in every job, in every organization, *must* result in something the organization needs. It has to be something that can be detected and measured.

Some work products are pretty obvious and it's easy to tell whether they're what they're supposed to be. They're generally things you can see, hear, smell, taste, touch—hair dryers, tubas, perfumes, candy, valves, medicines, reports, graphs, etc. It's usually pretty obvious if they ended up being what they were supposed to be, were produced on time, were delivered where they should have been, etc.

It can be much trickier though to tell if other types of work products or services are what they were supposed to be. Customer service is like that.

What are customer services reps supposed to produce? What results can you observe and measure—see, hear, touch, etc.—when a customer service task was been completed successfully? What work results were expected, and how can somebody tell if they've been produced? These kinds of results are not as obvious as physical objects you can see, hear, touch, etc.

*A supervisor **must** be able to define what a good work result is in observable, measurable terms, no matter how hard that may be.*

However, regardless of what the work task is, supervisors and employees have to be able to tell if the product or service that results "passes muster." Can the result be measured and is it what was asked for?

If a supervisor can't clearly define a work result in measurable terms, or can't tell clearly if it has been produced or not, then how can that supervisor expect any employee to produce "good" work? Employees can't hit a target they can't see.

A supervisor *must* be able to define what a good work result is in observable, measurable terms, no matter how hard that may be. Without a clear definition of the expected work result, a supervisor really has no grounds for holding anyone accountable for producing it.

So that's the WHAT—employees have to know what they're being asked to produce.

How do Bosses and Coaches compare on managing the WHATs?

With the Bossing approach, the Boss decides what the employees should produce and communicates that clearly to them.

With the Coaching approach it is actually *no different*. The Coach also decides exactly what the employees should produce and communicates that clearly to them.

So in terms of deciding what work results the supervisor wants and communicating that clearly to the employees, there's no significant difference between Bossing and Coaching. Bosses and Coaches both have the same responsibility to decide what's to be produced and to communicate that clearly to the employees.

How About the HOW?

Knowing exactly what results are expected is absolutely necessary for producing them. However, just knowing that doesn't necessarily ensure good results. A person also has to know *how* to produce them.

People have to have the necessary skills and abilities to do the job. They either come to a job already equipped with those skills and abilities, or they have to learn them through some sort of training.

They also have to know how to *apply* those skills and abilities to get the expected work results. They have to have the goods and know how to use them.

That's basically the HOW—employees have to *be able* to produce the work results they're being asked to produce.

As I said above, although there is no difference between Bossing and Coaching when it comes to managing the WHATs of a job, there is a *huge* difference in the way they manage the HOWs.

Bossing

Bossing (big "B") is the traditional way of supervising I talked about earlier. It's the one that's been handed down from supervisor to supervisor for generations.

It's been adopted by many, many supervisors because it's basically what they learned from their supervisors, who learned it from their supervisors, etc. Because the Bossing approach has been passed down so consistently over time, it's common for supervisors to adopt it without much thought or question.

Bossing is a top-down, command and control, do-as-I-say way of supervising. With this style of supervising, the Boss holds the ultimate control over the HOWs of getting jobs done.

The employees do the work, but the Boss pretty much controls how they do it. The Boss has the final say when it comes to the HOWs.

Bosses tend to believe they are the ultimate authority on how to get things done. They usually believe they succeeded so well before getting promoted because they knew the best way to get things done. After all, they ask, if their way wasn't really good, would they have been promoted to supervisor in the first place?

So, the Boss is the one in control of matching up HOWs with WHATs. The Boss looks at what has to get done, decides how it should be done, tells the employees to do it that way, holds their feet to the fire to do it that way, and comes down pretty hard on them if they don't. The employees' job in all that is to simply listen to the Boss and do as they're told.

Bosses don't tend to ask for employee opinions or ideas about how the job should be done. If employees do happen to have an idea for changing the way a task might be done, they can't just change what they're doing. They have to first ask permission from the Boss. If the Boss likes the idea, he or she will okay it and probably tell all the other employees doing that job to change the way they're doing it accordingly.

If there's a change in the WHAT—a change in direction, or a change in a product spec for example—the Boss figures out how the employees should change the way they do their work. If a process breaks down, the Boss takes charge of figuring out what's gone wrong and tells the employees how to change what they're doing.

Bosses tend to believe that all the employees are, or should be, equally capable of doing the same work tasks in the same way. They can have a pretty low tolerance for anyone who doesn't do things "right."

The Boss will tend to blame performance failures on employee attitudes, motivation, intelligence, etc. Since everyone is given the same directions for how to do the job, it must be the fault of the employee if something goes wrong—right?

Bosses discourage, and at times even *forbid*, employees from acting on their own. If something isn't going right with the work, the employee is supposed to check in with the Boss for instructions for what to do about it. If an employee does happen to take the initiative to solve a problem and fails, the Boss's reaction is usually pretty negative, and it's made real clear that next time they're supposed to come to the Boss for direction first.

So with the Bossing approach, managing the HOW—the way something should be done—is under the control of the *supervisor*. It's the Boss who ultimately decides how the job should be done, and expects the employees to all do it that way. The *employee* is to simply pay attention to exactly how the Boss wants things done and do it that way.

Coaching

Controlling the HOWs is the major defining difference between Bossing and the Coaching. Whereas the Boss maintains control over the HOWs of getting any job done, the Coach wants to give as much control as possible over how a job gets done *to the people who are actually doing it*.

Like Bosses, Coaches clearly communicate the WHATs to employees. But *unlike* Bosses, Coaches share with the employees the decision making about how those WHATs get done.

"I want employees to manage their own jobs so I can manage mine!"

Coaches don't have, and don't even want, total control over how everything gets done. They want employees to have as much control as possible over managing their own HOWs.

The Coach wants the employees themselves to take responsibility for looking at the relationship between the WHATs and HOWs of their jobs. They want employees to be constantly looking at the connection between what they're being asked to produce and how they're producing it

Coaches want employees to continuously pay attention to the way in which they're doing their work impacts the work results they get. The Coach wants the *employee* to become the expert on the relationship between the WHAT and the HOW.

Bosses will often say, "You're not getting paid to think!" Coaches believe just the opposite. Coaches *want* employees to think about what they're doing.

A rallying cry of Coaches is, "I want employees to manage their own jobs so I can manage mine!" A Coach's basic viewpoint is—let those who are doing the work manage the work. Coaches want employees to *own* their jobs and to manage them as much as they can by themselves.

Coaches constantly work on developing employees' *competency*—knowing what results are being asked for, and doing what needs to be done to produce those results. Remember how developing employees to be competent is a cornerstone of the supervisor's *role*?

Coaches and Bosses both want employees to be engaged in their work. Bosses think they simply need to demand it. Coaches, however, believe that you engage employees by giving them the knowledge, abilities and *control* they need to manage the HOWs to meet the WHATs. So, Coaches constantly develop employees' abilities to do just that.

Before You Freak Out!

Coaches don't give up *all* responsibility for the HOWs and simply hand over full control, lock-stock-and-barrel, to the employees. No, no.

Coaches educate employees about what they can and can't change on their own. They make sure employees know what rules and procedures are not up for grabs. They clearly describe the boundaries within which employees can operate independently. They allow employees to go ahead and manage their work within those boundaries without having to ask the Coach's permission first.

Coaches teach employees how to analyze work situations and identify what is working, and what isn't, for producing desired work results. Coaches give employees a lot of *freedom* to figure out the best way to get something done and then allow them to go ahead and do it.

> *When an employee doesn't get the desired work result, Coaches don't berate the employee.*

They ask for employee ideas and inputs about how to get things done. They want employees to constantly be thinking about what they're doing and whether it's working for, or against, getting the desired results.

Coaches teach employees how to problem solve and how to choose the best solution. When an employee doesn't get the desired work result, Coaches don't berate the employee. Instead, they help the employee think through:

- What happened.
- Why the result wasn't acceptable.
- Analyzing what he or she did that didn't work.
- Identifying what should be done instead next time.

Coaches see almost every interaction with employees as an opportunity to help them learn how to manage their own jobs. They help employees understand and own the HOWs of their jobs.

The essence of the difference between Bosses and Coaches is *control* over the HOWs—who's got control, how much do they have and how do they use it. Bosses have just about all of it when it comes to deciding how things get done. Coaches share as much of it with employees as they can responsibly handle.

Let's look at why this control thing is so important.

5 CONTROL

You may at this point be saying, "Well yeah, okay, Bossing and Coaching look at control differently. What's the big deal about whether the supervisor or the employee has control?" Well, it turns out to be a *very* big deal indeed!

A lot of supervisors believe that giving up any control over how employees go about getting a job done is a wide open invitation for trouble—errors, scrap, rework, inefficiency, etc.

> *Without going out of compliance with any written procedures, there are still subtle—or in some cases not-so-subtle—differences in how employees do a job.*

Chaos is the word many supervisors use to describe it.

In the face of all the standardizing of procedures that's erupted in organizations over the past decade or so (like certification by ISO-whatever, Lean Manufacturing, etc.) it can be really hard to accept this idea of giving some control and responsibility for deciding the *how* to employees.

So much of how any job is done has become dictated by detailed procedures that are written by the organization, certified by some agency or another, and audited by that agency for compliance. It can lead to feeling like there just isn't any wiggle room at all for allowing individual differences in getting a job done.

Watch Closely

I'm not going to tell you to ignore or throw out written, standardized procedures—seriously I'm not. They play a very big and important role in helping ensure quality, customer satisfaction, efficiency, etc.

What I *will* say though, is that everything isn't as wired as you may think. Without going out of compliance with any written procedures, there are still subtle—or in some cases not-so-subtle—differences in how employees do a job. For example:

- How they hold their tools
- Where things are located on their desk or workstation
- Whether they use their left or right hand
- How they touch, move, set, position, or hold products, raw materials, pieces/parts, etc.
- Whether they refer to written instructions, job-aids, checklists, etc., and if so, how often

I know for a certainty that I can observe any two people doing "exactly" the same job for just a few minutes, and will quickly be able to start listing differences I see in how they're doing that job. I know because I've done that very thing many times over the years.

Wherever and whenever employees can find any option, big or small, for how to do something, they'll generally put their own spin on it. They'll tend to do it in a way that works best for them. And they're really good at finding options amidst a pile of written or verbal procedures. Nothing evil going on here. It's just human nature to try to find ways to do things that are easier for the person doing them.

So you may say, "But shouldn't I do whatever I can to keep employees from doing that—adding their own 'spin' to how they do things? Shouldn't I work really hard to control how things are getting done and make sure everybody is doing everything *exactly* the same way to prevent the *chaos?*" Well, here are some things to think about.

Don't Tell ME What To Do!

Remember saying that as a kid? What a hassle it was to be told what to do by adults, other kids—anybody. We all go through that phase, and in fact most of us never get out of it entirely. I don't believe there are many adults who actually really *like* being told what to do. Some may resist it far louder than others, but I think we're all pretty much hard wired to want to be independent and do what we want, when we want, however we want to do it.

So telling employees exactly how a job should be done in great detail tends to stir up a bit of that natural resistance in them. People want to feel free to do things *their* way and yet here they are, being *told exactly* what to do, whether they agree with it or not, like it or not.

Most of us realize we have to give in a bit—or a lot—if we're going to do something someone else wants us to do. In our personal lives, we usually have a choice whether we'll give in and do it or not. In a job, though, we've agreed to give in to what the organization tells us it wants done—it's in the contract I talked about earlier between the organization and the employee.

If employees want to keep working for their organization, they have to produce what it tells them to produce. So they do it, although sometimes begrudgingly. But, just because employees agree to produce *what* the organization tells them to produce, it *doesn't* mean they won't tend to resist being told exactly *how* to produce it.

So even though they've agreed to the contract, most employees still don't much like being told how to do things all day long. It's just human nature for people to resist being *controlled.*

That's a large part of why employees respond so much better to Coaches than Bosses. Coaches understand that natural resistance and allow employees some control over how they do their job.

How About Motivation?

In every workshop I've conducted over the past twenty years supervisors have asked me, "How do I motivate my people to just do their jobs?!?" Often at least half the supervisors in attendance express that frustration.

> Most people are far more motivated to do something when they're allowed to choose the way they'll do it.

I'm going to talk about the significant role *control* plays in employee motivation.

I said earlier that an employee has to know how to get a job done. However, very often (in fact I'll say almost *always*) there is more than one way to get most anything done.

When you want to get something done outside of work, you can almost always come up with more than one way to get it done while still producing exactly the same result. Often you'll have a way to do it that you prefer over other ways you can think of. It's usually a way that's easier, more comfortable, more enjoyable, or faster for you.

Having some control over how you'll do something motivates you more to do it than if someone else is "forcing" you to do it a different way. Most people are far more motivated to do something when they're allowed to choose the way they prefer do it.

If two employees are expected to produce *the same result*, but each is allowed as much room as possible to do it their own way, they'll each be more motivated to produce that result. On the other hand, if they're each forced to do it exactly the same way, one or both of them is going to be less motivated.

The more people are allowed to do something their way, the more motivated they'll be. The more they're "forced" to do something in a particular way, the less motivated they'll be. It's just human nature.

Living Proof

Here's an example for you. My wife and I are both capable of mowing our lawn. We're each able to produce the same end result—all the grass cut to the same length over the entire lawn.

I like to mow by cutting *very* straight rows, equally spaced, over the entire lawn. I also rotate the direction of my lines forty-five degrees clockwise each time I mow to prevent getting "nappy" grass. When I'm finished, the lawn shows a nearly perfect pattern of straight, criss-crossing lines—just like a professional baseball field. It's a beautiful sight to my eyes, indeed!

My wife, on the other hand, goes at it with what seems to me to be a nearly random approach. She wanders here and there, almost as if the mower is pulling her around wherever it wants to take her, hitting-or-missing clumps of grass with each pass. She eventually gets all the grass cut, but her lines look like a disorganized mess to me—and let's not even talk about "nappy" grass!

When I mow, all the grass gets cut to the same length. When she mows all the grass gets cut to the same length. Same, same. We both achieve the desired result—all the grass cut to the same length all over the entire lawn.

As long as we get to mow our own way, we get the same end result—all the grass is cut to the same length—and we are each willing (motivated) to mow.

But what if we weren't allowed to do it each our own way? What if we were forced to mow the lawn the way I do? That still works fine for me—I'm still motivated to mow. But I'll tell you right now with absolute certainty that if this requirement were added, my wife would *not* mow the lawn. (I know because she told me so!) She is now unwilling (unmotivated) to mow.

As long as they're producing the desired results, let them do it their own way as much as possible.

You see what's going on here? If we change the rules so that her way is no longer allowed, she's unmotivated to mow—simply because we've taken away her *control* over HOW to do it.

The point to all this is that, if you want employees to be as motivated as they can be to do something, allow them some control over how they do it. As long as they're producing the desired results, let them do it their own way as much as possible.

Now obviously, if allowing an employee some control over how to do their work results in an unacceptable result, then that employee *can't* be allowed to continue doing it the way they're doing it.

But, *if* an employee is producing the required results, while having some control over how it's done, that employee will be more motivated to continue producing those acceptable work results.

It's Not a Free-For-All

Let's be clear, though—there are some key "rules" that apply here.

Rule 1—The exact specifications for the end result must be *very* clearly defined and communicated to the employee by the supervisor. There has to be no doubt in an employee's mind exactly what the end result needs to be.

Rule 2—The employee has to produce what they're expected to produce. It has to meet all the requirements for an acceptable end result. If an employee's way of doing something results in anything other than what is required, then that way is not acceptable.

Rule 3—They can't break any regulations such as safety rules, written procedures, policies, schedules, quality standards, etc. If an employee believes a written procedure is actually not the best way to do something, they can't just ignore it and go their own way. They have to go through proper organizational channels to get it changed.

Rule 4—Doing it their own way can't make it more difficult for anyone else to do *their* job. You don't get to blow my day up because you found a way to make your day better!

As long as those four rules are followed, then let employees have as much control as possible to find ways they prefer for doing the work. Let them have the freedom to figure out the best way to get the results you expect. The more control they have the more motivated they'll be.

Simply put, more control means higher motivation.

Coaching lets employees have some control. Bossing doesn't. As a result, people who work for Coaches are generally pretty motivated. People who work for Bosses generally aren't.

Want Some Free Process Improvement?

Here's another good reason to let the employees have some control over how they do things.

If you're like most people, you have regular chores at home you have to do. Taking out the trash, doing the laundry, buying groceries, feeding the dog, driving kids places, cleaning the house. Things you "have" to do on a regular basis.

Let me ask you this—do you ever look at one of those chores and say to yourself, "Man-o-man, it's taking me *two* hours to get this done. That's ridiculous! There's *got* to be a way I can stretch it out to at least *four* hours!"

Or, "It costs me twenty bucks every time I do this. No way! I'm going to find a way to get it closer to thirty or forty bucks at least!" Probably not, I'm guessing.

There's GOT To Be A Better Way!

We're always looking for easier, faster, less expensive ways to get our chores done, right? We want to spend less time and money on chores and have more time and money for having fun!

Well, which do you think a job is like more—doing chores, or having fun? Oh, there may be some fun in our job, but no getting around the fact that it is work. After all, somebody has to pay us to do it, right? I believe a lot of us wouldn't do the job we're doing right now, at least the parts we don't particularly enjoy, if it weren't for the money.

So a job for most people is like doing chores. And if we have a natural tendency to find ways to make chores faster, cheaper and more efficient at home, why wouldn't the same thing hold true in our jobs?

Because most employees find their jobs to be a lot like doing chores, they'll *naturally* come

If supervisors allow the employees to have as much freedom as possible to do things their own way, process improvements will occur as a result—naturally, automatically.

up with ideas for how to do their jobs faster, easier, more efficiently—on their own, without additional incentives from others.

If supervisors allow the employees to have as much freedom as possible to do things their own way, process improvements will occur as a result—naturally, automatically. You don't really need fancy continuous improvement programs and reward programs to encourage employees to find better ways to get things done. They'll be motivated to do it every day, on their own.

Coaches do this. Bosses don't. Processes tend to continually improve a lot under Coaches—automatically. Not so much for Bosses.

One for the Road

Here's yet another good reason to ease up on controlling everything and giving some to the employees instead.

By controlling everything, the unintended message Bosses send is that employees aren't smart enough to figure things out on their own. It says they can't think well enough to see what needs to get done and figure out the best way to do it on their own. It says their ideas aren't much good for anything.

As a result, employees feel insulted and resentful. They don't try to use their heads because they're treated as though they don't know how. They're *not* motivated to take their jobs seriously, to own them. There's no incentive to improve how they do them.

On the other hand, the message a Coach sends employees is that they *are* smart. It says that employees *are* capable of using their heads. It says they're smart enough to analyze what needs to get done, analyze the situation, and figure out acceptable, intelligent ways to do it.

As I said earlier, you as a supervisor get what you expect. If you expect employees to think, they will. If you expect them not to, they probably won't. Thinking employees do better work. Thinking employees improve things. Thinking employees make fewer mistakes. Thinking employees are *motivated*.

Coaches believe employees are intelligent enough to handle having control responsibly and effectively. Another reason why employees reporting to Coaches are more motivated than those who report to Bosses.

And Finally...

If having motivated employees who are engaged, making constant improvements, and largely managing themselves isn't enough, check this out.

CONTROL

Employee Productivity:

If a Boss does a really good job of Bossing—making it clear to employees what they are to produce and making sure they all do it exactly as the Boss says—then the Boss will get pretty high productivity from employees.

If a Coach does a really good job of Coaching—making it clear to employees what they are to produce, and giving employees some control over managing their own jobs—then they, too, will get pretty high productivity from employees.

If we stopped there, then there's not much to argue for one approach or the other. Bosses and Coaches can get good productivity by Bossing or Coaching well. *BUT*...

Absent Supervisor:

If a Boss has to be away from the workplace for any period of time, productivity starts to take a dive. The longer the Boss is away, the deeper the dive.

If a Coach has to be away, productivity stays pretty high—no matter how long the Coach is gone.

Now why would that be?

Well, people who report to Bosses have been told in no uncertain terms not to act on their own. They're told the Boss will always tell them what to do.

When a Boss is absent, the pressure is off for a while. Nobody hovering over them micro-managing how they're doing things, watching their every move, scolding them if they're not doing something "right."

If anything should happen to go wrong while the Boss is away—like trouble with equipment, missing or flawed raw materials, or any other unexpected problems—the employees have no choice but to stop what they're doing and wait for the Boss to get back to tell them what to do.

On the other hand, when a Coach is away and something goes wrong, the employees can usually handle things on their own because they know how to manage their jobs. They know how to troubleshoot and problem solve on their own. They don't need to wait for the Coach to return in order to handle most things that crop up.

As long as nothing ever goes wrong, or the supervisor never has to be away from the work place then either style should work. But things *do* go wrong, and supervisors *can't* always be present. (most managers spend 65% to 95% of their time in meetings, *not* in the workplace).

Employees keep working well when Coaches are absent. Not so for Bosses.

Employee Morale:

And finally, the morale of people who report to Bosses is generally not very high. The morale of people who report to Coaches is generally quite high. How come?

Well, if you are basically told you aren't capable of thinking intelligently, have to do things one way even if you see a better way, get dressed down for any mistakes you make whether or not it was your fault, can't improve anything at all about your job for even just your own comfort, and have to endure somebody controlling your every move—all the conditions imposed by Bosses—how could you have anything BUT low morale?

Alternatively, if you are treated as if you are a respected, intelligent, motivated and skilled adult, given the control to take charge of your job and get things done effectively, and taught the skills to handle problems right away on your own—as a Coach would treat you—don't you think your morale would be pretty high? Of course it would be.

The Lesson in All This?

Well, if you want to be a Boss then go ahead and be one. But...manage the WHATs and the HOWs very well, don't ever leave the workplace, and don't complain about employee morale.

On the other hand, if you want to be a Coach—go for it. Be a good one, though. Develop employee competency at managing their jobs. Explain the WHAT very well, do a good job of letting the employees help figure out the HOW, leave the workplace whenever you need to, and enjoy being around employees with good morale.

Sounds like a no-brainer, doesn't it?

6 SO HOW DO I DO IT?

It's not so much how you *DO* it. It's how you *BE* it.

There are some techniques for Coaching for sure. But Coaching isn't just a matter of using certain techniques. It's deeper than that. It's an overall orientation and dedication to a particular style of supervising. It's how you see yourself as a supervisor—what it *means* to you.

"Being" a Coach refers to the personal beliefs you have about leading and developing employees, and how those beliefs guide what you do and how you act as a supervisor. Those beliefs lead to such general habits as:

- Maintaining a positive, supportive learning environment.
- Encouraging employees to try new things.
- Encouraging employees to take calculated risks.
- Helping employees learn from their mistakes.
- Setting an example for self development.
- Believing in employees' capacities for growth.
- Developing employees directly.

Actions like these sum up the way a Coach goes about being a supervisor. They show a general orientation to treating employees with respect, believing in them, developing their competencies. Coaches do these things directly and intentionally—day in, day out.

That's what *being* a Coach means.

Let's Get Specific

Out of that general orientation to *being* a Coach there's a specific, very powerful thing that Coaches do *all* the time. It's at the very core of how Coaches coach. They continuously, reliably, perpetually *ask employees questions*.

The gist of just about any work-related interaction between a Boss and an employee entails the Boss *telling* the employee something. Almost always it's the Boss either telling the employee WHAT to do, or HOW to do it, or both. (Surprise, surprise—sound familiar?)

It's pretty much a *one-way* "conversation." Boss talks, employee listens (hopefully!).

However, when a Coach interacts with an employee about something work-related, there's something very different about that interaction. About the only time a Coach gets into *telling* is when there's a need to tell the employee something about the work results that are expected.

Otherwise, a Coach will turn almost any work-related conversation into a question-and-answer session. A coach asks questions about the employee's understanding of the expected results, how the employee plans to get the task done, what resources the employee will need, etc. The purpose of these questions is to find out whether the employee clearly understands what needs to get done and has an acceptable plan for doing it.

So with a Coach, it's almost always a *two-way* conversation, because the employee has to actually respond to the questions.

Bosses *tell*. Coaches *ask*.

There Comes a Time

Although Coaches use this Q&A technique in just about every work related interaction they have with employees, there are four *outstanding* opportunities for a Coach to put this technique to work:

1. Giving assignments

2. Answering employee questions

3. Handling employee mistakes

4. Dealing with problem performers

Opportunity 1: Giving an Assignment

When giving an employee a work assignment, a Boss pretty much says something like, "Get XYZ done by the end of the shift, and here's how I want it done." The conversation then typically ends there and the employee is expected to go off and just do what the Boss said to do.

A Coach, on the other hand, will start with something like, "I need you to get XYZ done by the end of the shift," and then will immediately shift to asking the employee questions such as:

- "How do you plan to go about doing that?"
- "Where are the things you'll need to get that done?"
- "When do you think you can get started on it?"
- "What do you need to have to do it?"
- "Any questions about why it needs to be done by end of shift?"
- "Do you have any questions about the assignment before you head off?"

It's important for the Coach to know if the employee understands the assignment and has an acceptable plan for doing it. So to find out, the Coach goes a step or two beyond telling the employee what needs to get done and asks the employee questions. Coaches will tailor their questions to the situation—it's a brand new assignment, the employee looks confused, this kind of assignment is something the employee has struggled with in the past, etc.

By listening to the employee's answers to these kinds of questions, a Coach can tell whether the employee:

- Really understands what needs to get done.
- Has a plan that will likely produce the desired results.
- Knows what tools, resources and materials they're going to need.
- Knows where to find them.
- Is going to wait too long to get started.

- Understands how long their plan will realistically take.

- Understands the reason for the deadline.

- Is confused about the priorities for what needs to get done, and when.

I think you'll agree, it's far better to find out up front whether an employee understands the assignment than it is to wait until a mistake happens that shows you they actually don't. You want to check with them beforehand, to make sure they don't head off in the wrong direction and fail.

The only way to know if the employee really understands the assignment is to find out what they're thinking about it. The only way to know *that* is to get them to tell you what they know and what they intend to do. The best way to do that is to *ask them questions*.

Opportunity 2: Responding to *Their* Questions

How many times a day do you find yourself having to respond to employees asking *you* questions? If you're not sure how often, try this.

For just a half a day carry around a pencil and a small piece of paper. Every time an employee comes to you with a question, just put a small tick mark on the piece of paper. Don't be obvious about it—this is just for your own use. At the end of that half-day, add up the tick marks on your paper.

I guarantee you'll be surprised how many tick marks you have after just four hours.

You're responding to questions all the time. If you're like most supervisors, many of those questions are ones you've answered many times already.

A lot of their questions are about what they should do, or how you want something done. Or they're asking you to solve a problem for them—a machine is down, a co-worker is bothering them, they can't find something, somebody isn't giving them something they need, etc.

Look at how much time you spend every day answering questions the employees should have the answers to themselves, or could easily find on their own. Look at the time you spend every day solving problems for them that you really wish they would just solve on their own.

Where's That Come From?

What you're experiencing is most likely an artifact of people having a history of being supervised by a Boss. The Boss tells people what to do, how to do it, and when to have it done. The Boss has all the answers. If there's any question about what to do or how to do it, ask the Boss. If you are at all uncertain, ask the Boss. If you can't remember, ask the Boss. You aren't allowed to fix things on your own, so ask the Boss.

So it's no wonder you get all the questions you do. As you can see, this is something that's programmed into them if they've been supervised by Bosses—and most of them have been.

You're not really doing yourself or the employees any favors by *always* answering their questions. When you do that, employees learn they can pretty much count on you any time they want an answer. That means they don't have to remember answers themselves, or figure them out on their own. It means basically that they don't have to *think*.

If you want to turn that around and work with employees who *do* think, who can answer most of their own questions, and who can solve most of their own problems, then the Coaching technique of asking questions is the way to get that. Here's how you do it.

Not All Questions Are Created Equal

There's one very important, overriding rule for asking questions—don't ask questions that can just be answered with a simple *yes* or *no*. Why?

For one thing, most of those yes or no questions are really *answers* disguised as questions. "Did you look in the file cabinet?" is actually an instruction to go look in the file cabinet. "Did you ask Bob?" is actually an instruction to go ask Bob.

Instead of yes-or-no questions, always ask what are called open-ended questions.

For another thing, a yes-or-no answer doesn't really tell you anything useful.

For example, if I were to ask you if you had any questions about what I just said, and you replied, "No," how do I know whether you *really* understand what I just said?

Maybe you just want me to go away and leave you alone. Maybe you're too lost to even know what to ask. Maybe you really *think* you understand what I said, but in fact you don't. From a simple "No," I can't tell whether you really understood what I said or not.

On the other hand, if you said, "Yes," what does *that* tell me? Nothing really. "Yes" doesn't give me the slightest clue about what you actually understand.

With either a "yes' or a "no" answer I'm going to have to ask more questions to find out what you actually do, and don't, understand. I gain nothing with a yes/no question. It's much better and faster to just start with the kind of question that gets a meaningful answer in the first place and not waste my time or yours starting with a useless yes or no question.

So What Do I Do Instead?

Instead of yes-or-no questions, always ask what are called *open-ended* questions. That means the employee has to answer with more than just a simple yes or no.

Questions that begin with WHO, WHAT, WHEN, WHERE, WHY, or HOW are open-ended. Yes or no can't be logical answers to those types of questions. They require fuller, broader answers. An open-ended question gets a response that's more like a complete sentence rather than just a single word.

Suppose an employee comes to you and says, "What do you want me to do next?" and you know the answer is actually on a schedule prominently posted in the employee's work area. Rather than just giving the employee the answer, or telling them where to look, you would instead ask something like:

"What are your thoughts on what you need to do?"

Or, "Where can you find that answer yourself?"

Or, "If I weren't available right now, how would you find the answer to that question?"

By asking these kinds of questions instead of just giving the answer, you're:

- Making employees *think* about what needs to be done, which helps them learn to manage their jobs on their own.

- Breaking their habit of coming to you for answers when they're capable of finding the answers on their own.

- Saving yourself the amount of time you have to spend repeatedly giving the employees answers that they should either know, or can find on their own.

- Helping employees learn how to problem solve.

- Showing the employee that you *believe* they are capable of finding their own answers.

- Creating a respectful environment where employees can believe in themselves and grow.

How About Some Examples?

There are a lot of questions or problems employees bring to you—machine failures, lost tools or paperwork, coworker personality conflicts, forgotten passwords, forgotten procedures, etc.

Here are a few examples of questions you might use for handling some of those issues:

Who have you checked with?	Where was it last time you looked for it?
Who used it last?	What does the manual say?
What does the SOP say?	What have you tried so far?
What did you do last time?	How have you done it in the past?

Where might that be written down?	What did you use before?
If I weren't here what would you do?	What tools can you use instead?
How's that quality look to you?	What have you asked them to change?
How does that impact you doing your work?	What can you do instead?
What are others doing about it?	What are you doing that might be causing it?
Why do you think that might be important?	What do you understand the priorities to be?
What did the customer say?	Where haven't you looked yet?

And that's just a few of them to get you started. Coaches develop an arsenal of these types of questions. Over time you'll find yourself coming up with a pretty good list of your own. As with other things, practice will make you perfect, so just keep working at it.

Remember, what you're trying to do is to *help* them. You're helping them come up with the correct answer on their own whenever possible. You want *them* to take responsibility for managing their jobs. That means being able to find answers on their own as often as they can.

Keep It Real, Though

I'm not saying employees should *never* ask you questions. If you're the only one who has the answer, then it's appropriate. If they're new to the situation and really don't know the answer yet or how to find it, it's appropriate to give them the answer.

I'm talking about when they really *should* know the answer because they've heard it before, or the answer is readily available to them without your help. These are the times that try your soul and eat up so much of your time and attention. Here's where a Coach's practice of responding with questions can pay off in spades.

Over time they'll stop asking you for answers they already know or can find. They won't want to keep going through this Q&A process if they don't need to. They'll eventually learn that it's much easier for them to just answer their own questions whenever they can.

If you discover they *can't* find the answers, then this Q&A process will help you understand why they can't. It gives you an opportunity to *teach* them something about being resourceful and managing their jobs. It's a great opportunity to *coach* and develop them.

A word of caution here—don't come across like you're making fun of them, talking down to them, or treating them like they're stupid. You shouldn't act like a smart aleck or be sarcastic. Remember, the goal here is to help them develop their ability to find answers on their own as often as they can. You want to show them you're confident they can do that. Be sincere, and this technique will work wonders.

I Dunno

There are some "dodges" employees may use to try to derail this question-and-answer thing you're doing. These are often attempts to get you back into just giving them an answer. That's sometimes easier for them than having to answer your questions.

The first dodge is the "I don't know" answer. It's possible an employee really doesn't' know the answer or where to find it. But it's also possible the employee is just trying to take the easy way out. It's easier for them to just get you to give them the answer.

It's important for you to find out what the employee really does and doesn't know. If the employee truly doesn't know the answer, then it's appropriate to give it to them—*this time*. But if they should know the answer or where to find it, then you need to get them to stop relying on you and start finding the answer on their own.

What you're after here is not letting an "I don't know" stand. Often an employee will be hoping this nips your Q&A in the bud. It's sort of like they're hoping that if they say they don't know the answer you'll quit asking them for it.

However, you want the employee to know that they are *expected* to know the answer. Keep asking the employee about what they don't know, and why, so you can help them figure out the answer on their own. Go back to the arsenal of questions you've been developing and keep on asking!

Another version of "I don't know" is "I forgot." You don't want to fall into telling the employee the same thing over and over because they "can't" remember it.

If you find that happening, then it's time to say something like, "You seem to be having trouble remembering this. What do you think you can do to help make sure you remember it from now on?"

How Can I Help?

A second common dodge is the dreaded *"La Brea Tar Pit"* of the Q&A game—asking the employee, "How can I help?"

Down you go! They immediately start thinking things like, "Yes, thank you *very* much for asking! You

I know you're a caring person who wants to help employees succeed, but you don't do that by doing their job for them.

can figure this all out *for* me, or maybe even just *do* it for me!" Isn't that a special turn of events? You just opened the door wide for them to delegate solving their problem back to *you*!

I know you're a caring person who wants to help employees succeed, but you don't do that by doing their job *for* them. They have to be able to do it by themselves—it's *their* job

If they ask directly for you to do any of the thinking or the actual work yourself, then first say to them, "I can't really do that *for* you—that's not my role here." Then shift gears into asking questions like, "What are your thoughts about what *you* can do on your own to handle it?" Go back to your arsenal of questions and redirect the conversation to what *they* can do.

By helping them learn to manage on their own, you're actually giving them the *best* help you can. You help them by ensuring they can help themselves.

What??

I've saved maybe the biggest dodge for last. It's when an employee says to you, "What are you asking *me* for?" I have supervisors telling me all the time how common it is for employees to respond to their questions this way.

They may think it's *your* job as supervisor to have all the answers and that it's their job to just do as they're told. That's how it goes with a Boss, but not with a Coach.

You need to explain to them that their job is to know what they're expected to get done and to do it. *Your* job is to do whatever you can to help them do that *on their own*.

Let them know why you're asking them questions. Tell them it's really important they know the information they need to have about their job, or know where they can easily find it.

They need to know you're expecting them to be able to do their job without having to come to you for information they can find on their own. You're expecting them to manage their own work well. Your questions are designed to help them develop the ability to handle more things on their own.

Once you've explained what you're doing with the Q&A and why, you can then go back to asking your questions.

This Q&A business can be a disturbing turn of events for employees—especially if they've had a lot of experience working under the Bossing style. It's important for you to assure them that this isn't a trap, or a game.

They need to know that you understand this may be freaking them out a little, but that the whole intent is to help them grow their abilities to work on their own as much as possible. It's also a good idea to explain how this will make it easier for them to succeed in their jobs and take some personal pride in that.

So—avoid those common "dodges" you're likely to encounter. If they really don't know the answer—help them learn how to find out. If they want you to just answer their question or solve their problem for them, then explain to them that the best way for you to help them is to teach them how to handle these things on their own. If they think it's part of your job to know everything, then remind them that it's *their* job to know everything about their own job and your role is to help them gain that knowledge.

Opportunity 3: Dealing With Employee Mistakes

An employee's mistake can be really upsetting. It seems like no good can ever come of it. And, if you're a Boss, that's pretty much a true statement.

There's just no good reason to berate the employee.

If you're a Coach, however, it's a different story. For a Coach it's not *all* bad, actually.

Nobody likes mistakes, nor should they. Mistakes screw up quality, schedules, equipment, and budgets. They often make management unhappy, and *you* get to take the brunt of that unhappiness.

A Boss will tend to react *negatively* to an employee's mistake—getting angry, coming down on the employee, casting blame, scolding, threatening. The Boss's approach to the whole thing is pretty much to blow up and tell the poor offending employee that it had better not happen again or else!

The result for that employee is often embarrassment, shame, anger, resentment, etc. The more it was an "honest" mistake, the worse the employee generally feels. Lots of negativity and uproar, but one serious lack—no targeted, effective *learning* about how to not make that mistake again.

There's just no good reason to berate the employee. It only serves to make an already bad situation worse. Employees seldom learn anything positive from being intimidated.

Coaches don't like mistakes any more than anyone else. But, Coaches don't view an employee's mistake as a reason to come down hard on the employee.

Instead, a Coach first makes sure the employee recognizes and acknowledges that in fact a mistake was made, and what that mistake was. Next the Coach gets right to the business of helping the employee, in a positive way, figure out what happened and what to do differently next time.

A Coach views a mistake as a *learning* opportunity for the employee. Coaches work with the employee to analyze what was going on, and figure out what might have been a better thing to do in that situation.

Not only does the employee learn a different approach to that situation in the future, but maybe even more importantly, the Coach has just helped develop that employee's ability to analyze a situation, come up with various actions they might take, and choose the best one. It's an excellent opportunity to develop employees' problem-solving abilities, which in turn develops their ability to manage their job in general.

So What Questions Do You Ask Here?

Here is a generic process I strongly recommend you walk the employee through. It's a process that's fairly common among a number of popular problem-solving and decision-making models. The process has five steps, each involving questions for the employee to answer:

1. **Appraise the situation—what happened and why?**
   - What was going on—what did the employee see and hear?
   - What did the employee think needed to change?
   - What did the employee do?
   - Why did the employee choose to respond the way they did?

2. **Identify a number of alternative actions the employee might have taken instead.** What alternative actions might have been considered?

3. **Evaluate the pros and cons of each alternative and choose the one that seems to be the best to address that situation in the future.**
   - How well would each alternative have fixed the situation?
   - Are there any downsides to each alternative?

4. **Observe the results.** When that situation arises again, evaluate how well the action chosen in Step 3 worked this time. If it worked—great! You're done.

5. **If that solution didn't work, have the employee look at:**

   - What alternative might work better?

   - Why would that alternative be better than the other options?

   - Could that alternative actually be implemented?
   - Does it have any undesirable downsides that would rule it out?

If necessary, continue cycling through Steps 1 through 5 until a satisfactory solution is found.

Each of these five steps involves asking the employee questions to get them to think about what happened, what might be a better way they could handle that situation next time and why.

You can see how going through this process with the employee ought to leave them with a better solution for handling the situation next time. It also (maybe even more importantly) teaches them a general process for solving problems that has an excellent chance of helping them avoid making mistakes in the first place.

Man, That Could Take Some Time!

It can be hard in the emotion of the moment to take the time to have this kind of conversation with an employee. It can be difficult to stick to asking questions and not just *telling* them what to do next time.

However, it's essentially a time-investment scheme. If it's done correctly, this one-time process actually results in a tremendous rate of return on time invested. A *little* extra time spent up front saves a *lot* of extra time down the road.

> Spend a little time now, or a lot of time later—simple as that!

A Coach will spend less time *overall* dealing with a mistake because all the time that would have had to be spent repeatedly dealing with that same mistake over and over again is saved. Done correctly, this approach means that mistake doesn't keep happening, so less time spent overall.

Spend a little time now, or a lot of time later—simple as that!

Not only that, but the time spent in that one discussion develops that employee's ability to solve problems on their own as new situations arise. That is another great time saver for the employee as well.

If you follow this procedure, and do it in a true spirit of helping the employee learn how to handle problem situations better, then I guarantee you'll get really good results. You'll see fewer mistakes, better work results, much better problem prevention and much greater employee competency.

And just to sweeten the pot further, I'll toss in this little addition to the equation—you'll see much higher employee *morale*, too! They'll make fewer mistakes and gain greater self confidence.

Opportunity 4: Dealing with Problem Performers

This topic tends to be a universally hot one for supervisors. Trying to figure out how to deal effectively with a problem performer can be one of the most frustrating challenges any supervisor faces.

In fact, this topic is big enough, and important enough, that I'm devoting *all* of Part 4 to it. I'll show you how *coaching* can bring you the greatest chance of resolving the problem once and for all.

Before getting into that, however, I need to talk about how to communicate effectively. Knowing how to communicate with an employee is very important. Knowing how to communicate with a problem performer is *critical*. It needs to be done right. So I'll talk about communicating effectively with employees before I move on to confronting a problem performer.

PART 3

COMMUNICATING EFFECTIVELY

In Part 1, I covered *what* the role of the supervisor is—adopting some key mindsets and producing competent employees. In Part 2, I covered *how* to do that best –Coaching and not Bossing. In Part 3, I'm going to cover communicating effectively.

Why? Well, to be effective as a supervisor you have to be able to explain clearly what you want employees to produce. And if you're going to be an effective Coach, you have to be able to ask them good questions and understand their answers.

All that requires you to communicate well.

Most people seem to assume a supervisor who successfully communicates expected results, and asks good questions, is communicating pretty well. Although those two feats are each critically important, effective communication doesn't stop there.

Being able to *listen* is an equally, if not *more*, important skill in communicating effectively.

There's an old saying, "We're given one mouth and two ears, and we ought to use them in that proportion." It turns out, however, that most of us aren't good at *real* listening, despite what we think.

Research has clearly shown that it's physically impossible to talk and listen at the same time. It's also been shown that most of us would rather talk than listen. That means there's a lot of talking going on and not much listening.

So even though most of us think we're pretty good listeners, the research tells us that we aren't really. This has a pretty significant impact on supervising effectively.

I've covered the importance of knowing what employees think. And I've shown you how to ask them questions to find out. However, if you aren't able to listen carefully to what they're saying, you'll never know. If you're not able to listen, you're not able to communicate.

Part 3 will cover:

- How to communicate your messages clearly to employees.

- How to *listen* well to employees.

- How to get employees to listen to *you*.

7 THE FACTS OF THE MATTER

Communication is a very present topic in most, if not all, organizations. I've been involved in creating and administering employee surveys for over forty years, and have noted that communication has been a problem area in virtually every survey I've ever conducted. People just aren't very good at communicating—especially in organizations.

Now, I don't want to hurt anybody's feelings here, but truth be told, *most* of us are pretty bad at communicating. Oh, we all may *talk* a lot, but we don't really *communicate* very well. Nothing personal, it's just something experts have consistently found to be the case.

Why's that? Well, research has uncovered some key reasons.

So Much to Say, So Little Time!

The first reason is one I just mentioned—people are generally more interested in talking than listening.

"Not me!" you may say. Well, do you ever:

- Make premature comments or evaluations?

- Interrupt others when they're talking?

- Mishandle being interrupted ("Hey, I'm *talking* here!")?

- Dominate the discussion and not let others have equal air time?

- Repeatedly tell others what to do whether or not they asked you to?

- Argue excessively?

- Display irritating listening habits (no eye contact, answering the phone while someone is talking to you, reading something that's not part of the conversation, completing sentences for the other person, etc.)?

These are pretty typical signs that you're more interested in talking than in listening. So, if you catch yourself doing any of them...

As I've said, it's been *proven* that people can't talk and listen at the same time. So while we're doing the things I listed above, we aren't listening—we physically *can't* be.

Even if we're not talking out loud, most of us are constantly busy "talking" inside our heads. All the while someone is talking to us, our minds keep drifting off into our own internal conversations— working up an argument, or deciding if we agree with the speaker, or thinking about how good their hair looks, or planning what we're going to pick up for dinner tonight, or thinking back to how well we bowled last night, or how our shoes are too tight, or...

> *We have to be equally, or **more**, interested in listening than we are in talking.*

So when an employee is talking to us, we're often very busy talking inside our heads. That's still *talking* and that means we're not listening.

If everybody's talking, then *nobody* is listening. If nobody's listening, then communication isn't happening, plain and simple.

To be able to communicate effectively we *have* to be able to close our mouths, tune out our own thoughts, and devote our full attention to what an employee is saying to us. We have to be able to quiet our busy-box minds and focus our attention intently on what's being said to us. We have to be equally, or *more*, interested in listening than we are in talking.

Finding Just the Right Words

The second reason why people don't communicate well has to do with our tendency to focus on words alone to communicate what we're trying to say.

It's a very good idea to pay attention to what we want to say and the exact words we want to use to say it. We often figure that, if we choose our *words* carefully and wisely, we'll send the message we want to send.

However, research has shown that a big problem is that those words we have so painstakingly chosen only convey about *seventeen percent* of the total meaning we're trying to communicate—at *best*.

WHAT?? How can that be? Where's the other eighty-three percent?

Well, it turns out that the words we use are only a minor part of the total meaning we actually convey. The majority of what we communicate is conveyed by what's called our "body language." We communicate a great deal through non-verbal behaviors—subtle movements, posture, facial expressions, volume, tone, eye contact, hand gestures, etc.

Eighty-three percent of what we're telling someone has nothing to do with the words we're using. *How* we say things is actually much more important than *what* we say!

If you question whether that's possible, just look at how you can get so much more meaning out of seeing an actor speak lines in a play than if you just silently read the script to yourself. Or look at the *huge* range of ideas and emotions a good mime portrays—with *no* words at all!

So to communicate effectively with an employee, you have to give them access to more than just your words. You have to let them pick up on your non-verbal language as well. That means at least hearing your voice, as in a phone call, or actually seeing you face-to-face.

While I'm at it, here's a little side thought for you. Let's look at emails, written memos and written announcements for a second.

What do these communication methods contain besides words? *Nothing*!! That means the best-crafted email or memo can only convey seventeen percent of the message you want to send. This is even scarier when you stop to consider the huge reliance on emails and written communications that is so prevalent in all organizations.

If you want to communicate anything other than something really simple and straightforward (like "Take a fifteen minute break."), then you've *got* to at least give employees the benefit of hearing your voice if not actually talking to them face-to-face.

The more important the information and/or complicated the message, the more critical it is to not just rely on words, but to send it live and in person.

Taking the Slow Train

The third reason we don't communicate well has to do with a little physiology.

The average person talks at a rate of about 140 words per minute. So that's the pace of most conversations.

However, we *think* way faster than that. So we mentally process things being said to us much faster than they're actually being spoken.

Remember that tendency to talk inside our head? Well, while we're trying to wait patiently for the speaker to get their message across at 140 words-per-minute, there's all kinds of room for our lightning-fast, busy-box minds to take over and redirect our attention to other thoughts.

So here we have another compelling argument for us to learn to shut our minds off when an employee is talking to us and focus our attention entirely on what they're saying to us—no matter *how* long it seems to take. You can't listen well if your attention is busy being elsewhere inside your head.

A Faulty Recorder

A fourth reason why we aren't good communicators has to do with memory.

Research has shown that when we're actually *trying* to pay attention to what someone is saying to us, we'll only remember about fifty percent of what we just heard—*immediately* after it was said! Worse yet, after two or three days, we will remember only about twenty-five percent of what we heard!

> *So simply telling an employee to just listen up and pay attention means they're only going to remember somewhere between ten and fifty percent of what you said.*

But wait, it gets worse. If we *aren't* really paying attention to what someone is saying to us, we'll only hang on to about thirty-five percent of what was said immediately after it's said, and after a couple of days that number drops to ten percent!

So simply telling an employee to just listen up and pay attention means they're only going to remember somewhere between ten and fifty percent of what you said. Not their fault—they're only human.

If you were to ask an employee, "How many times do I have to tell you?" I guess the answer is clearly—more than once!

Here again, you can see the importance of asking employees questions to find out what they actually heard. That gives you some hope of being able to find, and fill in, the fifty to ninety percent of your message they didn't get.

If you only tell employees to pay attention and then drop your message on them, you have no reason to be surprised or upset if it doesn't seem they heard a thing you said. Not their fault. It's just how it is with people and you have to work *with* that, not against it.

It's Not Hopeless, Though

As you can see, communicating effectively is not an easy thing to do. However, I've shown you that there *are* ways to overcome some of the major challenges. When you're communicating with an employee:

- Curb your desire to talk.

- Close down your own thoughts when they're talking to you.

- Avoid relying solely on written communications for important messages.

- Speak face-to-face as much as possible.

- Attend fully to what's being said to you.

- Say important things more than once, maybe in different ways.

Next, I'm going to show you how to get your message across as clearly as possible. Then I'll show you how to be an excellent listener, and how to help *employees* to be good listeners, too.

8 SENDING YOUR MESSAGE

Here's a basic dilemma in trying to convey a thought to an employee—you already know what you're trying to communicate, but they don't. You're embarking on a mission to get whatever is in your mind into theirs, and that's a tricky thing to accomplish.

Why?

Well, one reason is that you might be struggling with getting your own thoughts together, or finding the right words. Some examples are:

- The "tip-of-the-tongue" phenomenon.
- The momentary memory lapse over a word or phrase.
- The "I can't find the words" experience.
- The "I don't know quite how to put this" lament.

If *you* can't get what you're trying to say straight in your own mind, how can you possibly expect to plant it correctly into *theirs*? Not gonna happen. There's no sense even trying until you've got it straight for yourself first and know how to verbalize it.

A second reason is that your way of verbally expressing a thought may not be a way the employee relates to. We all have our own characteristic ways of putting words and sentences together that aren't necessarily how others do it.

We each have our own vocabulary that makes sense to us. We have our own pet words and phrases for things. (When I worked for a golf course, I was once told to "Go hook up the artificial wazz to the grey goose and do seventeen." Say *what?*)

There are regional differences in what things are called (is it a pop, or a coke, or a soda?). Those can make it difficult for an employee to understand exactly what you're saying.

An employee who's not familiar with the words you're using, or how you're using them, is lost at sea, clueless.

A third reason is that we tend to create mental "shortcuts" for combining several related thoughts into one-word labels to keep it simple for ourselves. For example:

- Lazy
- Tasty
- Hard
- Interesting
- Fun

It can be real useful for *us* to have these categories of thoughts all bundled together into a single word or phrase in our own minds, because for us, a single word can encompass a whole special array of related thoughts. But others may have their *own* bundles of related thoughts that are conjured up by that word, and the two bundles don't necessarily match.

For example, you can tell someone you always use "a blend of Italian spices" on your pasta. But how could they possibly know exactly what spices you put together and in what proportion? Your pasta and theirs more than likely aren't going to taste the same.

Using a single word or phrase to convey exact meaning to an employee can be completely futile. Not surprisingly it can lead to some pretty big misunderstandings!

If you really want an employee to understand the thought you're trying to communicate to them you need to stop relying on your own personal "shorthand" way of talking. You need to make the effort to spell things out for them in as much detail as they need to really grasp what you're saying.

This business of getting a thought out of your head and into an employee's is tricky, for sure. But it's not hopeless. Using the general suggestions to communicating I'll give you next, it should go much better, for *you* and for the *employees* with whom you're trying to communicate.

Some Suggestions for You

Here are some thoughts to keep in mind whenever you're trying to communicate with an employee:

1. **Know how to shape your message in the way the employee likes to receive it.**
   If your job is selling pencils, and your sales territory is in Italy, you'd be well-advised to speak Italian to potential customers, and not English, if you expect to sell very many pencils. Speak in the employee's "language."

   If the employee you're talking to wants big picture, then give them big picture. If they want details, give them details. If they don't understand certain names and phrases your organization uses, don't use them in this instance. Your job is to make sure they understand what you're saying, so you *have* to say things in ways *they* understand.

2. **Take your time.**
   Don't bowl them over by giving them too much information too fast. Pause frequently to let them "catch up." Check in with them to see if your pace is working for them. If they're catching on quickly, speed up your delivery. If they're lagging behind, slow down.

3. **Find out how you're doing.**
   The temptation is to keep barreling through what you've got to say until you're finished. But, you may have left the employee in the dust early on and everything you said after that was wasted. Clues that this has happened could be a confused look on their face, they're trying to interrupt you, they're looking away, etc. Stop every now and then to see what they've understood so far, or if they have any questions. That way you can keep them with you until you reach the end of what you're trying to say.

4. **Don't overdo it, or underdo it.**
   Some employees need more information than others, some less. It's usually a function of how familiar they are with the subject you're talking about. Learn how much information a person needs and adjust your presentation accordingly.

5. **Know what you're trying to say before you say it.**
   I've touched on this already, but it bears repeating. If you don't know what you're trying to say, how on earth will the listener figure it out?

SENDING YOUR MESSAGE

Take the time to get your message straight in your own mind before starting to talk. If you need some time to do that—take it.

Believe me, you won't be saving any time by launching into a conversation before you're ready. You'll not only have to spend extra time talking until you get it right, but you'll also have to spend even more time straightening out all the confusion you created by not being clear in the first place.

9 MESSAGE RECEIVED...OR MAYBE NOT

"Any questions? No? Okay, go get it done!"

The employee got the message—or did they? Did they really understand what you said? Not just your words, but the *meaning* behind them as well?

You may feel like you've done a masterful job of communicating your thoughts just like you wanted to. And you may have done that—to *your* satisfaction.

But what about the employee? Did you successfully *communicate* with the employee? Did they get the message you wanted them to? Maybe, maybe not.

> *You have only communicated successfully when the employee gets the message you intended to send.*

Two big assumptions are in play here. One is your assumption that what you said and the way you said it were very clear. The other is the employee's assumption that they clearly heard exactly what you said.

As we saw in the previous chapter, one or both of those assumptions can *very* easily be wrong. And you usually won't find out whether either, or both, of those assumptions are wrong until later when something ends up going haywire, and it becomes painfully clear the communication somehow failed.

You have only communicated successfully when the employee gets the message you intended to send. Easily said. But how do you know if they got your message accurately? Not always so easy to tell, is it?

So, What to Do?

First, send your message as clearly as you possibly can. Is your message clear in your own mind? Are you able to find the right words? Are you speaking in a way the employee can understand? Are you giving them an opportunity to pick up on all your non-verbals? All the things I talked about in the previous chapter for being clear in your delivery.

Second, you need to find out what the employee heard. Is it what you were trying to say?

If the conversation simply stops when you're done talking, you can't know for sure what they thought you said. They may nod, or look perplexed, angry, or happy…but their facial expressions don't tell you much at all about *what* they actually heard.

How can you find out what they heard? Well, there are a couple of ways.

One is to watch what they do after you're finished talking to them. Does what they do next show they understood you? Or do they head off in the wrong direction and do something completely out of sync with what you just said?

That can certainly tell you whether you got your message across to them successfully. Unfortunately though, it happens *after* the fact. If they didn't understand you, it can result in mistakes, unintended outcomes, wasted resources, lost time, and hard feelings for you and for them. And it also means you'll now have to take the extra time to go back and try communicating your message again. Clearly not a very efficient or positive process!

A better way is to get them to talk to you. Get the employee to talk about what they heard right after you're done saying it—before they go off and do *anything*. Does what they tell you they heard match up with what you were trying to say? Did they get your words right but miss the meaning in some way? Does putting what they heard into their own words show they got your message?

That will not only tell you whether they understood your message, but it will also help ensure they've got it right *before* they take any actions. Problem prevention is always better than problem recovery!

So, if you want to get an employee to reflect back to you what they think you said, how can you get them to do that?

So Tell Me...

The simplest way to get them to talk to you is to (yes, here it is again!) *ask them questions.*

You see, most employees will pretty much just sit or stand there quietly while you're talking to them. They may ask you a question or two to clarify something. But that's usually pretty much it. For the most part employees tend to be quiet, inactive and minimally involved in the conversation.

It probably won't surprise you to hear that this is very common in a Bossing situation. The Boss's job is to tell an employee what to do, and the employee's job is then to simply go off and do as they were told. It's pretty much one-way communication and not much interaction goes on.

When an employee is just quietly listening, you really have no idea what, if anything, they're actually *hearing*. They may be looking at you and nodding, but not really taking in anything you're saying. Or they may be "hearing" what they *hope* you're saying.

They may be lost inside their own minds, putting together plans for after-work, or wondering where you buy your shoes, or watching someone walk by behind you. And even if they are actually taking in your words, there's no way to really tell if it's making any sense to them at all if they remain quiet.

The only way to really know what they thought you said was to get them to talk to you. And that usually means you have to ask them questions.

Back to the Basics

Earlier, in the section about Coaching versus Bossing, I talked about the kinds of questions a Coach asks and I explained about avoiding yes/no questions. You'll recall the problem with those is that they really don't tell you much.

"Do you understand what I'm saying?" "Yup." Do they, though?

All a "yup" means is that they either *think* they know what you said, or that they want you to just go away now and leave them alone. It tells you *nothing* about what they understood, or what they didn't.

Instead of yes/no questions, you want to tap into basic open-ended questions that typically begin with:

1. ***WHO***
2. ***WHAT***
3. ***WHEN***
4. ***WHERE***
5. ***WHY***
6. ***HOW***

You'll remember that hese kinds of questions can't be answered with a simple yes or no. They require a much larger, more informative answer. By listening to the answers the employee gives to these questions, you can get a pretty good idea of how well they understand what you were saying.

So an example of making a statement and following it up with questions might be:

"Good morning, Alice! I'd like you to put together a report on the status of the Barlow project for tomorrow's staff meeting."

And then follow up with questions like these:

"***Who*** do you think you need to coordinate with?"
"***What*** all do you think you'll need to include in the report?"
"***When*** do you think you can have a draft for me to review?"
"***Where*** is the information you're going to need?"
"***Why*** might anyone take issue with this report?"
"***How*** can you best work this in with your other priorities?"

Another example might be:

> "Bob, I have to ask you to switch over to the Product A Line and crank out 1000 units before the end of the day."

Possible follow up questions:

> "*Who* will you need to work on this with you?"
> "*What* raw materials are you going to need to gather?"
> "*When* will you need to get started?"
> "*Where* are the spec sheets you'll need?"
> "*Why* might this be tricky to get done on time?"
> "*How* do you plan to go about getting it done?"

Some of the answers you get may show you that the employee doesn't completely understand what you want them to do. They may overlook someone who needs to be involved, leave out important resources, plan to start too late to get it all done, etc.

These would all be signs that they didn't understand something about what you said. If that's the case, you can then get it straightened out with them right away before they hit trouble somewhere down the line.

If the employee's answers show they really do understand what you said, then off they go and you can rest fairly well-assured that things will go well.

What Do You Understand?

At some point it may become clear during all your questions that the employee just doesn't understand what you're saying. If so, it would be appropriate for you to simply ask the employee what they do understand you to be saying.

You need to find out what the employee is missing or misinterpreting. If you were to simply keep repeating yourself over and over you're not going to get there. What you need to know is what did the employee hear, and look for where the misunderstanding happened.

What you need to do is *carefully* get the employee to repeat back to you what they understood you to say. I say *carefully* because you don't want to come across as being sarcastic, or putting them down, or treating them like they're stupid.

> *You have to be careful not to insult their intelligence or seem sarcastic.*

You might say something like, "It seems like you and I are getting our wires crossed on this one. I might not be doing a very good job of expressing myself, here. What do you understand me to be saying to you?

Again, the important thing is to find out why there's a difference between what you're trying to say and what they're hearing. You want to do that in a way that makes it obvious you're not coming down on the employee, but honestly trying to make sure you're both on the same page.

It could be something in your delivery, it could be something they're just not picking up on, or—most likely—some of each. Seek to understand, not to blame.

You have to be careful not to insult their intelligence or seem sarcastic. Remember, it's your responsibility to make sure they do understand, so a little humility on your part will go a long way.

10 ACTIVE LISTENING

Okay, so an employee is talking away at you, and you're *sure* you know what they're saying. But do you *really*?

Remember all the problems with communicating I described earlier, such as only retaining 50% of what you hear immediately after hearing it, or the tendency for your mind to wander because your brain processes information at a much faster rate than the 140 word-per-minute speaking rate you're listening to?

> *Employees need to know you're listening to them and taking them seriously.*

Well, with all that going on it's actually pretty likely that you *don't* know exactly what the employee just said to you. You may have some of it correctly, but not all of it by any means.

When an employee is talking to you, it's *imperative* that you grasp what they're saying as accurately and completely as you can. If you're not *really* listening to them you won't understand what they know and think, and without that you really aren't in a position to ensure they're going to be successful.

Not only that, but employees can quickly tell if you're really listening to them or not. If they pick up that you're not, they'll predictably shut down and quit trying to talk to you. Obviously no good will come of that. It's an open door to resentment and mistakes.

Employees need to know you're listening to them and taking them seriously. One of the best ways to show them that you are is known as *active listening*.

So What You're Saying Is….

The vast majority of us tend to engage most of the time in *passive* listening. That means we're looking at the other person, maybe nodding now and then, but not saying anything. When that person is done talking (or when we interrupt them), we launch immediately into whatever it is *we* want to say.

With *active* listening, rather than launching right into what *we* want to say when they've finished talking, we first check with the other person to see if what we thought we heard is, in fact, what they were actually trying to say. We don't get into saying what *we* want to until we first "get the nod" from them that we did hear them correctly.

That gives them an opportunity to let you know whether or not you really heard them. If you didn't, they can try to clarify what they're saying before the conversation goes any further.

The whole goal with active listening is to either get a confirmation that you heard them correctly, or allow them a chance to clarify what you missed. You do that by reflecting back to them what you heard to see if you got it right. "Is this what you're saying?"

What It Is, and Isn't

Active listening is all about paying close attention to what an employee is saying to you and really hearing what they're trying to tell you. It's making a very conscious, and obvious, effort to get their complete message—not just the words they're saying, but also the meaning and emotion behind their words.

Active listening *IS*:
- Giving good eye contact.
- Putting your own thoughts on hold.
- Showing appropriate facial expressions (nodding, smiling, etc.).
- Asking questions about what they're saying to get clarification.
- Reflecting back what you believe you heard.

Active listening is *NOT*:
- Interrupting them.
- Planning your own response to what they're saying.
- Being judgmental.
- Agreeing or disagreeing with what they're saying.
- Trying to solve their problems for them.
- Venting your own emotions.

Active listening is all about understanding them, and holding off on your own reactions or responses until it's clear that you do. It's about focusing on them, and not on yourself. You'll get your turn—once you know you're clear about what they're telling you.

Paraphrasing vs. "Parrot-phrasing"

The best way to check back with an employee talking to you is to put what they're saying into *your own words* and ask if you've gotten the message correctly. That is known as *paraphrasing.*

That is different from what I call "parrot-phrasing." This is when you just repeat their exact words back to them.

Parrot-phrasing can be helpful if you're not sure you *physically* heard what they said. It may have been said too softly, or it may sound too much like a different word to you.

But parrot-phrasing has its limitations. You can make sure you get their words correctly. But that doesn't mean you understand their words, or how they're using them.

Another limitation of parrot-phrasing is that the words they're saying may not match how they're feeling emotionally. An employee may tell you they feel just fine, but the scowl on their face and the gruff way they say it tell you they're not fine at all. If you just repeat the same words back to them, you're not conveying the emotional message you're picking up behind of those words.

On the other hand, putting what they just said into your own words by paraphrasing gives you a great opportunity to see if you not only heard the words correctly, but also the meaning and emotion behind those words. If you can paint a verbal picture a bit differently than they did and it still turns out to be the same picture, you've got it.

Show Me, Please

Here's a hypothetical example for you.

Suppose an employee said to you:

> "Man it really ticks me off that my report got ignored in that meeting. I put a lot of time in on it, and nobody even *looked* at it! What a bunch of jerks. Why do I even try?"

Using *active listening*, you would say something to them like:

> "So, sounds like you're pretty steamed and frustrated. You put a lot of time and effort into getting that report together, and it didn't seem to you like it got any attention at all."

So far, so good. But *is* it the whole message? What's behind calling them "jerks" and questioning why they're even trying? There's more being communicated here.

If you think there's more to what they're saying, you can then go further and speculate about what else is being said, to see if you're on-track with their *whole* message.

You could say something like:

> "It sounds to me like maybe it's not just the report that's bothering you. You also seem pretty upset with the other people in that meeting. It's like they disrespected or insulted you personally. It doesn't seem to you like you got any recognition for your efforts at all. I can see how you might be feeling frustrated with them and resentful. Is that kind of where you're at?"

What you're doing here is reflecting back to them what *you* understood their *whole* message to be. You're reflecting back what they seemed to be feeling and why they were feeling that way. You're checking in to see if you got their whole message correctly.

Just a Sec—I'm Not Sure I'm With You

Paraphrasing back what you heard an employee say is all well and good if you're pretty sure you heard what they said. But what if somewhere along the line you realize that you really don't understand what they're saying well enough to be able to paraphrase it? Well, it's time (oh no, not *again*!) to ask questions!

Here's a partial list of example questions you might ask to get the clarification you need:

- Could you say that again using different words?

- You said "his." Did you mean "her?"

- Could you give me some more information about that?

- Are you saying…?

- Is it *them*, or what they're *doing*, that's bothering you?

- Could it be you're excited about…?"

- Are you saying this happens to you a lot, or just occasionally?"

- Is it possible that…?"

What you're doing here is gently and politely asking a question or two so you can clear up any confusion or misunderstanding you may have. Again, you're asking questions for clarification only. You're not challenging or criticizing them.

There are some nice advantages to doing this:

- The employee doesn't have to guess why you don't seem to understand what they're saying.

- It may actually help clarify to the employee in their own mind what they're trying to say.

- It shows you're listening.

- It tells them you care about what they're saying.

- It may help them gain some insight into what they're experiencing emotionally.

- They'll learn that you are a good listener and will open up to you more.

So Listen Up!

Communicating well with employees is critically important to being a successful supervisor. They can't produce the results you want if you don't clearly explain what it is you want them to produce. It all starts there.

However, as I've said, communicating clearly *to* them is only part of the

> *Show them that you care about what they're thinking and that you want them to talk to you.*

equation. You also need to be able to *listen* to what employees are saying to you. It's the only sure-fire way to know what they do, and don't, understand about your expectations and what they need to do to meet them.

Use active listening with them. Reflect back to them what you understand them to be saying. Hold your own thoughts and comments at bay until you have that understanding. Show them that you care about what they're thinking and that you *want* them to talk to you.

PART 4

THE PROBLEM PERFORMER

Welcome to the home stretch! Here's where it all comes together.

I explained the role of the supervisor in Part 1—adopting some key mindsets and producing competent employees.

In Part 2, I showed you *how* to do that best—be an effective Coach and not a Boss.

Then in Part 3, I focused on communicating effectively. I emphasized how important it is not only to communicate clearly *to* employees, but maybe even more critically, to really *listen* to them.

Now in Part 4, I'll cover how to best handle a problem performer—a topic that is right at the forefront of most supervisors' brains. Sooner or later every supervisor encounters a problem performer. It's probably the most stressful and frustrating situation a supervisor can face.

And…it's a situation where everything I've talked about so far in this book comes together—working to make the underperformer COMPETENT, by COACHING them, using effective COMMUNICATION techniques.

I'll first talk about deciding if there really *is* a genuine performance problem. What they're doing may be annoying, but is it really a *performance* issue?

Then I'll talk about some very important mindsets I strongly suggest you adopt *before* you talk with an employee about their problem performance. If you've had much exposure to Bosses in the past, you probably have some "unthinking" to do.

Next I'll talk about the six possible reasons why employees don't do what you expect them to do. Every employee is different, but if they aren't doing the job it's due to at least one of these six reasons. I'll show you how to "diagnose" which of those reasons are causing a given employee's poor performance.

After that, I'll show you how understanding the causes of problem performance can provide you an "early warning" system for catching a struggling employee early and helping them get back on track *before* they turn into a problem performer.

Finally, I'll explain how to have "*the discussion*" with the problem performer. Not much fun to be had here, but it can be done with a minimum of upset for you and for the employee.

When you've finished Part 4, you'll be equipped to handle a problem performer as effectively as possible. Not only that, but you'll be able to help employees avoid becoming one in the first place.

At this point, I need to make an important point about organizational policies and documentation.

Every organization has procedures and guidelines for how to address performance issues with employees. There is a lot of variation among organizations for what to document, when, and how. As I said in the Introduction to this book, it's impossible for me to go over your organization's specific HR procedures and documentation requirements.

However, *if* you use the approach to the problem performer that I am recommending, you'll find it much easier and more effective to comply with your organization's HR procedures, no matter what those procedures look like. Every HR professional I've met who has looked at this approach has wholeheartedly endorsed it in light of their HR policies.

So, if you apply these concepts to handle a problem performer well, you will very likely not only see a significant improvement in their performance, but you may even be able to avoid having to even *start* your organization's formal procedures.

11 WHAT'S THE PROBLEM HERE?

Okay. You told them what to do. They didn't have any questions. You sent them off to get it done. And now you turn around and see that they're *miles* away from producing what you asked them to. What's going on here? Why can't they just produce the results you asked them for?

Most employees seem to be able to get their

There's a big difference between a problem and an annoyance.

job done to your satisfaction without a lot of prompting or hassling. Most of them will also experience the occasional glitch getting something done. That's normal and is to be expected. Nobody's perfect.

However, when those glitches aren't occasional but are instead the *norm*, it's time to find out what's going on.

Is It Really A Problem?

The first thing a supervisor needs to do is be sure there *really is* a problem. There's a big difference between a problem and an annoyance. Employees don't always act like we would like them to. They may do something differently than you do—arrange their tools differently, do a task in a different way, gossip with coworkers, organize a project differently, talk too loud, have tattoos, or whatever.

These things may bother you, but unless they're preventing an employee from producing the expected work results, or making it hard for another employee to get *their* job done, these are just things that annoy you, not work problems. You may not do these things yourself, but you have no authority as a supervisor to make the employee stop doing them.

What you *do* have the authority to go after are *work-related problems*. What's a work-related problem? Well, any time an employee is not producing acceptable work results, that's a problem. They're responsible to produce the results you ask them to produce. Not producing them just isn't in the options package. They *have* to get the results you're asking for. (Remember the *contract?*)

So, an employee not producing the expected work results is something you not only can, but *must,* address as a supervisor. It's your job.

That also means that, if they *are* getting the job done, not getting in anybody else's way, and not breaking any rules, they get to be who they are and do what they do, no matter how personally annoying it may be for you. You don't get to impose your will on them in matters that aren't *directly* related to getting their job done.

Before diving in and confronting the employee, make sure there really *is* a work-related problem and not just something you don't like or agree with personally. If you can show that the employee's work results are not in line with expectations, then by all means, go ahead and start dealing with it. But if the employee is producing the work results you're asking for, they are not a problem performer and you can't treat them as such.

Work Results, Not Behaviors

It seems to be easy for many supervisors to criticize how an employee *behaves.* They focus on what the employee is *doing,* not on their *work results.*

I often hear supervisors say things like the employee is:

- Goofing off.
- Wasting time.
- Showing a rotten attitude.
- Not paying attention.
- Chit-chatting with coworkers way too much.
- Just not taking the job seriously.
- Not pulling their weight.
- Not contributing to the team.

That may be how you perceive the employee, but these are all *behaviors*, not work results. You've *got* to focus first and foremost on work results because those are the WHATs you are holding them accountable for producing.

What employees are actually *doing* is only relevant as it affects their work results in either a positive, or negative, way. If they're producing good work results, their behaviors are fine. If they *aren't* producing good work results, then they're obviously engaging in some non-productive behaviors.

Now *you* may know that certain behaviors are behind the employee not producing the results you're asking for. But when talking with the employee, your focus needs to be on their poor *work results* when you're defining a work problem, *not* the behaviors you believe are causing the problem.

You want the *employee* to figure out which of their behaviors are keeping them from getting the work done. Your task is to facilitate them coming to that awareness *on their own*. That makes it clear to them that they're responsible for their own behavior, and it will have a much longer-lasting impact on their performance than if you simply told them what to do.

> *It's far better for **them** to identify what they're doing that's preventing them from producing timely results.*

So, for example, if you see an employee who's behind schedule in their work wandering around and not working on what you've asked them to, don't nail them for wandering around. Instead, talk to them about the fact that they're not meeting schedule.

Ask them what they're *doing* that may be causing that. Or, ask them what they need to do to start meeting schedule.

It's far better for *them* to identify what they're doing that's preventing them from producing timely results. It keeps *them* accountable for paying attention to why they're not getting the job done. It also reminds them that they are accountable for producing the expected *work results*.

Sooner or later they'll have to admit that wandering around instead of working is the reason they're behind. That keeps the focus on the work results you want, and makes them see the relationship between what they're doing, and the results they get.

So at first, focus only on work results. Don't focus on behaviors at this point. That will come into play later in the conversation.

Am I Clear?

If *you* don't know what results you want, or can't clearly tell whether you're getting them or not, how on earth are *they* going to figure it out? You're not ready to have a conversation until the work results you expect are crystal clear in your mind and you have clear evidence the employee isn't producing them.

For many jobs, it is relatively easy to come up with clear expectations and observable proof that the job is, or isn't, being done. For those jobs, it isn't too hard to compare what an employee is producing with what you expect them to produce.

Here might be some examples:

- "Bob, I asked you to produce 400 widgets a week, but here you can see that you only produced 258 last week, 340 the week before that, and 298 the week before that."

- "Alice, I asked you to get a monthly production report to me by the 25th of each month. Last month you got it to me on the 30th, the month before on the 28th, and the month before that the 31st."

- "Darwin, you should be making parts at, or above, the 98% quality mark. However, you can see from this report that your last batch was 75%, the batch before that was at 82%, and the one before that was at 93%."

- "Sean, I asked you to get at least 90% positive scores on your customer satisfaction surveys each week. These results here show you at 75% last week, 77% the week before, and 69% the week before that."

- "Camille, I asked you to conduct 15 audits a day. You can see here that you only averaged 12 per day over the past week."

You see how each statement begins with a *clear* statement of what the expectation is, followed by what the employee produced instead?

> *You have to get to the point where you can state clear, observable, measurable expectations for any job, no matter how easy that may, or may not, be.*

For some jobs, however, it can be a bit challenging to be that clear. The results may not be as cut and dried. For example, how can you tell whether or not an HR rep is doing their job? Or whether a customer service rep is doing their job? What are the observable, measurable work results for jobs like these?

You have to get to the point where you can state clear, observable, measurable expectations for *any* job, no matter how easy that may, or may not, be. Getting there may take some effort on your part, but you *must* be able to define your expectations clearly enough that you, and the employee, can tell for sure whether the job is getting done.

If you can't clearly define the results you expect, you can't hold an employee accountable for producing them. You *can't* have any conversation about whether or not they're doing the job because you have no concrete evidence to tell you one way or the other.

So if you can't state your expectations in concrete, measurable terms and find evidence whether those expectations are being met, you're *not ready* to have a performance discussion with the employee.

How Long Has This Been Going On?

When an employee who ordinarily gets their work done just fine falls down on the job and fails to produce what they should, they aren't *necessarily* a problem performer. If they get back up to speed fairly quickly and start getting their job done again, then they're just having a bad day—as we *all* do now and then.

However, when an employee shows a *pattern* of not getting their work done, then they are a true problem performer. They're not just having a bad day—they're having a bad work life! They're chronically failing to meet job expectations.

It's important for a supervisor to know the difference between an employee having a bad day and a problem performer. How you approach the employee will be much different for one versus the other.

An employee who's having a bad day needs understanding, support and encouragement. An employee who is a problem performer needs a wake-up call and a serious conversation. They need to recognize that there's a real problem going on and that they need to come up with a plan to get on—and *stay* on—track.

So, when an employee's performance falls below expectations, you need to look at their performance over time and determine whether this is just a blip or a trend.

If it's not a trend, you have an employee who needs your help. If it *is* a trend, you have a problem performer and you must confront them about solving their problem.

So to summarize, before you start a conversation about poor performance with an employee, make sure:

1. It's a *work-results-related* problem, not just something that "bugs" you.

2. You're defining the problem in terms of *work results*, not behaviors.

3. The results you want and the results you're getting are both very *clearly* stated in your mind.

4. You know whether you're looking at a "blip" or a trend.

12 WHY DON'T THEY JUST DO THEIR JOB?

It's enough to drive you right up the wall. It doesn't make any sense. Why don't they just do what they're *supposed* to?

Well, I'm going to give you six pretty good reasons. I refer to them as the "Big Six." I'll explain what those six reasons are and how to address each of them.

The "Big Six"

I'm going to ask you to take a few minutes and ponder the reasons *you* think employees don't do their job. Before you continue reading, jot those reasons down. In a bit, we'll come back to your list to see what you came up with.

Are you done yet? Okay. Let's take a look at why employees don't meet job expectations.

Reason 1: They don't know WHAT they're supposed to produce.

Wait a minute....how can *that* be? You've told them a thousand times already! How many more times do you have to tell them?

Well, at *least* one more. You *still* haven't said it in a way they can understand.

You see, no matter how clear you think you've been, there's a possibility that something is still missing in the translation for this employee. They may think they know what you want, but they actually don't. Maybe you're not communicating in a way they understand, or maybe they're just not listening very well.

Whatever the case, you need to keep working with them, using the techniques we covered in the communications chapters earlier. You have to find out what they're not getting. You need to get them to tell you what they believe you're asking them to do, and take it from there.

This can be frustrating for both you and the employee for sure. But if they really don't understand what you're asking them to do, you'll only get good results from them by accident, and that's no way to run a railroad. So be patient and be persistent.

Reason 2: They don't know HOW to do it.

Try as they might, they just aren't able to produce the results you're asking for. It could be:

- They're stuck in a loop, trying the same thing over and over without success.

- They need training from you or someone else who *does* know how to do it.

- They just aren't physically or mentally able to do it.

- It's confusing to them.

Whatever the reason, they can't produce what you want with their current knowledge and approach to the situation. You need to do whatever you can to help them become competent at that task.

You need to bring you're "A game" as a Coach. You need to talk to them, ask questions and observe them directly to help them figure out how to produce what you're asking them to.

If it becomes obvious they're just *not* going to be able to produce the results you want, then you need to be willing to back off on expecting them to do it. This job probably isn't a good fit for them. It just isn't something they're going to be able to do.

You need to work with HR to see if there is some other job they might be able to do in your organization. Or, it may actually be most realistic for them to leave your organization and find something more suited to their abilities elsewhere.

Reason 3: They don't know WHY you're asking them to do it.

Be careful now. "Because I said so!" is *not* acceptable (although many old-school supervisors still believe that to be the only answer they need to give!). They're confused about the *work—not* who's asking them to do it!

Adults are much more willing to do what you're asking them to do if they know why you want them to do it—even if they personally disagree with it. Just telling an adult it's "because I said so" is not in the least bit motivating. It usually makes them feel belittled, stupid, undervalued and resentful.

They need to know it's because those are the customer's requirements, or management has changed priorities, or there's a resource shortage, or there's a cost/benefit issue at the moment, or whatever it is. Give them the respect of telling them the work-related reason behind what you're asking them to produce.

One great benefit to telling them *why* is that they'll be more willing to do it. But, another *outstanding* benefit is that, if they understand the situation, they'll be in a position to maybe even help you meet the challenge by coming up with some suggestions of their own for how to get it done. Imagine that!

But what if *you* don't know the reason, either? Your management has simply told you what they want done without further explanation.

You're bound to be frustrated by that, but you have to fight any tendency to take your frustration out on those you are supervising. It's best for you to be truthful and simply tell them that you haven't gotten a firm explanation from your management yet. Let them know that you'll pass it on to them as soon as you do, and in the meantime you'll really appreciate their getting done what you are asking them to.

Reason 4: They don't have the RESOURCES they need.

Of course we all think immediately of material things when we think of resources. We think of tools, machines, raw materials, etc. And, of course, if they don't have the tools or materials they need, they're not going to get the job done.

But be aware that *time* is also a major resource. Ignoring the actual time constraints required to get something done, and telling an employee to just get it done anyway is really kind of stupid. They'll think so, and they'll be right.

Pressing employees to get things done when there really isn't time not only doesn't get the job done, it makes them really resentful and it undermines their trust in you. Why should they take you seriously when it looks like you really don't understand what it takes to get a job done?

Other employees are *also* a resource. If an employee can't get the job done without help, or they can't do it in the time frame you're giving them without someone to help them, they can't get the job done—period.

Employees need what they need. You just can't motivate employees to do their best when it's obvious to them you aren't being realistic about the resources required to do what you're asking them to do. You'll need to either back off on your expectations, or get them the resources they need.

Reason 5: There's something going on OUTSIDE WORK.

There's a problem in their personal life that's making it difficult-to-impossible to get their job done. They have a serious medical condition. They're going through a divorce. Their spouse lost their job. Their kid is sick. They hear singing and there's no one there.

I'm not talking here about just having the flu for a couple of days. I'm talking about something that's going to impact their work for a relatively long period of time. It may even be permanent in some cases.

There are some major "no-no's" for you to avoid in this situation:

No-No # 1. As a supervisor, you absolutely MUST avoid doing anything that is, or looks like, an attempt to directly help them solve their personal problem. If you try to help out, there's a very real possibility that

*Remember, you're a **supervisor**— period. You're not HR, a psychologist, physician, or attorney.*

you'll find yourself in some pretty hot water with other employees, with your management, with HR, maybe even with a lawyer or two. Not good.

That means do not:

- Give them advice about how to handle their personal situation.

- Suggest they take some time off work.

- Provide them personal counseling.

- Give them the name of your therapist.

- Suggest they go see a doctor.

- Refer them to your lawyer.

It may sound weird, and maybe even unfair, but when you do any of the above, you could potentially be accused by lawyers and other professionals of basically "operating without a license." You can be perceived as acting outside of your supervisory sphere of expertise, and in fact making judgments you have no authority or certification to make.

That won't go well for you. I've seen organizations land in court over these kinds of actions.

It can be hard to avoid helping an employee out, especially if you like them and hate to see them going through such troubles. But you *have* to resist. *You're* not the one to help them with such things. You may even just make things *worse* for them.

There are professionals whose job it is to help in these situations, and *they're* the ones to help the employee. Not you.

Remember, you're a *supervisor*—period. You're not HR, a psychologist, physician, or attorney. Don't get yourself in hot water by being accused of acting like one. Don't do anything your role as a supervisor doesn't specifically and directly authorize you to do.

What you *should* do, however, is immediately consult with your management and/or your HR representative to find out what they want you to do. Your organization has policies and procedures for handling these types of situations, and you need to follow HR's advice and your organization's procedures to the letter.

No-No # 2. Don't back off on your expectations for this employee's work results. You may be inclined to change the employee's job to something "easier" for them, something with what you perceive to be less pressure perhaps, to help them out. But don't do that.

For one thing, it smacks of your making a diagnostic evaluation that their job is too emotionally or physically stressful for them, which isn't something you are professionally certified to do. If this case ever ends up in court, there is a likelihood that the employee's attorney will claim you are operating like a therapist or a physician. Your job doesn't authorize you to do that.

For another thing, if you ease up your expectations for one employee, you necessarily are obligated to ease up your expectations for every other employee who has that same job. Treating employees *fairly* means you hold every employee in a job accountable for the same performance standards for that job. You can't make it easier for one and not for the others.

If HR tells you to do otherwise, do what they say—but understand *why* they're saying it.

Remember, the issue is that the employee is not meeting performance standards for their job. Changing those standards for just that employee is not the solution. You may decide to change the standards for everyone, but that seldom makes sense when you have just one employee who is struggling to meet expectations.

Reason 6: They just DON'T WANT TO.

They know *WHAT* you want them to do, they know *HOW* to do it, they know *WHY* you're asking them to do it, they have all the *RESOURCES* they need and life *OUTSIDE WORK* just couldn't be better (reasons 1 through 5 of the Big Six). They just simply *don't want to do* the work!

They may have explanations like:

- You don't pay them enough.
- They hate the job.
- Having to work for a living is grossly unfair.
- Work gets in the way of their leisure activities.

- It's too hot out.

- It's too cold out.

You've provided everything you can, and should, as their supervisor to enable

> *They have everything they need to do a good job except the willingness to do it.*

them to do an acceptable job. For whatever reason, they simply just don't want to do it, and will continue to not do it at every opportunity they find.

This is the *true problem performer*. They have everything they need to do a good job except the willingness to do it. I find it pretty remarkable that these employees will often spend more time, ingenuity and energy finding ways *not* to do the job than it would take to just *do* it!

How Did You Do?

So now take a look at the list of reasons you wrote down a few minutes ago for why people don't do their job. Where do each of the reasons you listed fit into the "Big Six" list?

What I consistently find in my training program is that most supervisors can come up with most of the six reasons. But I also find that most supervisors tend to list a lot of reasons that are actually just versions of reason number six.

Supervisors will list reasons like the employee:

- Is lazy.

- Has no work ethic.

- Has a rotten attitude.

- Feels it's all really unfair to ask so much of them.

- Is stupid.

- Feels entitled to their job whether they do it or not.

- Figures the world owes them a living just because.

- Is trying to get away with all they can.

- Retired some time ago and just forgot to tell anyone.

You can see these are all actually examples of the employee *not wanting to do* the job. So, the lists many supervisors come up with are often heavily weighted toward it all being the employee's fault—there's just something wrong with the *employee.*

Of course, there are obviously employees who just don't want to do the work for whatever reason. But putting the bulk of the blame on the employee misses a pretty key point. If you look back at that list, you'll see that fixing four out of six (*two thirds*) of the possible reasons an employee isn't performing to standards involves *you,* not just the employee.

You have a major role to play in fixing reasons 1 through 4 of the Big Six. You can't just blame the employee. It's not *all* their fault.

If the employee is unclear on WHAT you want them to produce, you're responsible for working with them to ensure they *do* understand.

If the employee doesn't know HOW to do it, you're responsible for coaching them and helping them learn a way to get it done.

If the employee is clueless about WHY you want it done, you're responsible for telling them.

If the employee doesn't have the RESOURCES they need, it's up to you to either make sure they have those resources, or to back off on what you're asking them to get done until they *do* have those resources.

Reason 5, something OUTSIDE WORK, is *not* your responsibility to fix directly, but you *are* responsible for seeing that company procedures for offering the employee help are followed. So even though you aren't responsible to help fix this one directly, you *do* have a role to play by following your organization's official procedures.

The last reason—they just DON'T WANT TO—isn't up to you to fix *at all*. It's entirely the employee's responsibility to fix this one. They've created a problem for themselves, and *they* need to fix it.

Your only responsibility here is to make it clear to them they can't continue to not get the work done and still expect to be employed by your organization. You have to let them know that they have a big *choice* to make—do the work, or leave.

This is your problem performer. This is the employee you'll have the "big conversation" with. I'll be showing you how to have that conversation.

Don't Jump the Gun

Even though it may be tempting to jump right off the bat to reason 6 and blame it all on the employee, you have to take a good look at what *really* is behind their not getting the work done. You have to check out the possibility that it's not just an unwillingness to do the work. There may well be something about the work itself that has them lost, frustrated or confused.

Accusing an employee of just not wanting to do the work, when in fact there is a legitimate reason outside their total control for their not performing, is a formula for disaster. You will have shot your credibility to pieces with that employee, and probably other employees as well.

It tells them you don't know, or care, about them enough to find out what problems they're having with getting the work done. They'll feel you're assuming it's all them and aren't even going to *try* to help them find a way to get the job done. Bye-bye trust! Bye-bye motivation!

You need to leave room in your thinking for the possibility (maybe even the *probability*) that there are one or more other legitimate causes for their poor performance. Be careful not to pre-judge that it's all the employee's fault and that they're a true problem performer before you've looked at the other five reasons.

How Did They Get There?

Very few employees start a job immediately deciding they won't do the work. Those few that do are typically out the door before the ink is dry on their employment papers.

Consistently poor performance usually happens over time. For one reason or another, an employee eventually loses the "spark" and gradually quits trying. Why's that?

Well, think back a bit. Have you ever been in a job where:

- You just didn't seem to understand **what** the boss wanted?

- Try as you might, you just flat didn't know **how** to produce the results your boss was asking for?

- You had no clue **why** you were being asked to do *that* when it seemed like you really should be doing something *else*?

- You just didn't have all the **resources** you needed to get the job done?

- Your life outside work was somehow making it very difficult for you to focus on your work?

Almost all of us have been in situations like these at one time or another. How did you feel when it happened to you?

Most of us can eventually get to feeling pretty *frustrated* if it continues. Now let me ask you—how do most of us usually express our *frustration*? Well, we usually act *angry*.

And what does an *angry* employee look like? They often look a whole lot like someone who is solidly stuck in reason 6—*someone who just doesn't want to do the job.*

So you see what happens here? An employee who really wants to do a good job and is trying hard to, ends up getting frustrated about not being able to do it.

If they can't get help, or figure it out on their own after going at it for some time, frustration and anger build until the employee just gives up and sinks into a state of just not caring anymore. A potentially great employee has been turned into a problem performer. Ouch!

"Well, why don't they just ask for help?" you might say. The answer is—they don't want to look stupid or incompetent. Especially if they have any history of having worked for a Boss in the past.

So they struggle along on their own, continuing to fail until they finally just give up trying. They eventually turn into a problem performer.

If only their supervisor had noticed early on that they were struggling and stepped in right away to help that employee. It could well have prevented the creation of a future problem performer.

13 IT'S MINDSET TIME AGAIN!

So, you've determined that you're faced with a genuine problem performer. There are two very important mindsets I suggest you adopt about dealing with a problem performer before confronting them and having "the conversation."

These mindsets may take a little while to sink in and become habit for you. They tend to go against some traditional ways of thinking that are pretty deeply ingrained for most supervisors. Those traditional ways of thinking are:

- The *supervisor* has the problem when an employee doesn't get the work done.

- Addressing a problem performer is a *discipline* process.

- It's usually an employee's attitude or motivation that's the reason they don't do the job.

Those traditional ways of thinking are not helpful. In fact, they're actually the cause of many of the difficulties supervisors face when they try to deal with a problem performer.

Break with those habitual ways of thinking and adopt the following mindsets, and you'll find dealing with a problem performer goes so much easier for you and for the employee.

Mindset One: Who's Got the Problem?

It sure feels like *you* do, right? Work isn't getting done, management is breathing down your neck, other employees are grousing. You're losing sleep and downing the antacids by the handful.

But you don't have the problem. It's the *employee* who has the problem. They aren't producing what they're supposed to.

Remember the contract? They aren't holding up their end of it and producing the results you're asking for, which creates a serious problem for them. They agreed to do the work in exchange for pay and bennies. If they don't do that work, their employment is at risk—no work results, no job!

> It's the **employee** who has the problem.

Now, in truth they don't *have* to do the work. But they can't stay in the job if they don't. If they choose to do the work, they are choosing to stay on the job. If they choose not to do the work, they're choosing to leave. Their choice. Their problem to solve.

That's not to say that their problem isn't *problematic* for you. Your management expects you to get results from the employees you supervise. When they don't, you're viewed as not doing your job. So, when your employees don't produce acceptable results, it creates issues for you. Your employee's problem is that they're not producing the expected results. Your problem is that *the employee* has a problem. If they solve *their* problem, then your problem is solved as well.

The big BFO ("Blinding Flash of the Obvious") here is that the responsibility to get the job done is the employee's. You can't do their job for them—they can only do that by themselves. You can help *them* come up with a solution to their problem, but you can't solve it for them.

That's a *very* important concept for you to keep in mind.

And it's *critically* important for the employee to keep that in mind. If you come across to the employee like you're the one who's having a problem here, it's guaranteed they'll then decide that it's *you* who needs to solve your problem. And you'll get responses like:

...they have a problem and it's their responsibility to fix it.

- Your expectations are way too high.
- You just don't understand their situation.
- You're having another bad day.
- You have it in for them for some reason.
- There must be something wrong in your personal life.
- You don't know how to supervise.
- Etc, etc., etc.

Sound familiar? See how they really don't think they have to do anything here, because it's *your* problem, not theirs? So they then decide that you need to change your expectations, be more understanding, get a life, etc.

Their take is—"You have a problem and you need to fix it!" Oh, and while you're busy solving your problem, why don't you just give them a break for heaven's sake and get off their back!

So the first mindset for you to adopt is—*they* have a problem and it's their responsibility to fix it. Your job is to facilitate their doing that and hold them accountable. Again, remember the contract.

Mindset Two: It's Not "DISCIPLINE"

This can be a fairly tough mindset to change. For years, organizations have used the word "discipline" in the title of their policies and procedures for handling problem performers. Many have changed to the more politically acceptable term, "corrective action," but the discipline mindset is still solidly buried underneath those words.

Seeing the handling of a problem performer as a matter of *discipline* is not the least bit helpful. You discipline kids and criminals. You don't discipline employees. You aren't their parent, and they haven't committed any crimes.

Rather than discipline employees, a Coach *facilitates* their solving their problem. A Coach works with an underperformer to help them find a way to consistently produce the desired results, using all the coaching techniques I covered earlier in this book. The goal of this problem-solving process is to help the employee find a way to reliably and consistently produce acceptable work results.

Okay, I get it, but what's the big deal about calling it *"discipline?"* Well...

Remember When?

You may possibly be an exception, but the vast majority of us got disciplined as kids. When you "broke the rules" or didn't do what you were supposed to do, you got disciplined in some fashion or another. You got a good talking to, and maybe more. It usually wasn't much fun to say the least.

IT'S MINDSET TIME AGAIN!

Think back to those wonder years. When you got disciplined as a kid, how did you feel? Most of us typically felt:

- Angry
- Resentful
- Embarrassed
- Frightened
- Maligned
- Picked on
- Sad
- Confused
- Vengeful
- Remorseful
- Unloved
- Mistreated
- Misunderstood

Those were the kinds of thoughts and emotions that were going on *inside* us as we were getting disciplined. How about on the *outside*? What did most of us physically *do* when we got disciplined?

We:

- Argued
- Pouted
- Cried
- Ran away
- Clammed up
- Vowed not to get caught next time
- Blamed somebody else
- Denied it all
- Told our parents they were unfair

- Lied
- Threatened retaliation
- Deflected attention away from ourselves ("Me! What about Bob?!)

Does all that sound familiar to you?

We learned from an early age how to react *emotionally* and *physically* whenever we were disciplined. And that learning has lasted long into our adult lives.

Now, think about "disciplining" an employee. What happens when they get disciplined? Do they seem to have the same *emotions* they had as kids? Do they seem angry, resentful, embarrassed, etc.?

You bet they do.

How do they *act* when they're getting disciplined? Do they tend to do the same kinds of things they did as kids? Do they argue, pout, cry? Do they "run away" (storm off in a huff, or call in sick for a couple days)?

Absolutely.

And we shouldn't be the least bit surprised. They're simply reacting to being disciplined the way they learned to as kids. It's hard-wired into them. It's unrealistic to expect them to react any other way even though they're adults now.

So, you coming at this with a discipline mindset will automatically bring out those emotions and behaviors in the employee—and that just isn't conducive to bringing about a positive, constructive outcome.

If you come from the mindset that this is *discipline*, the employee will pick up on that right away—you won't be able to prevent it. If the employee thinks you're going to discipline them, they'll respond just like they did as a kid—they'll react right away with negative emotions and behaviors.

When they respond negatively, it becomes a battle between the two of you. When it's a battle, one of you is going to win and the other is going to lose. When either of you loses, the performance problem doesn't truly get solved.

And…the negativity that occurs in the process will continue between the two of you beyond just the conversation. Perhaps worse, that negativity will most likely spread from you and that employee to the other employees in one fashion or another.

So the second mindset for you to adopt is that this is a matter of facilitating a *problem-solving* process with the employee and coming up with a workable solution. It is not a matter of "discipline."

With this *facilitation* mindset, you have a much greater chance of both of you acting like adults and focusing on finding ways to turn the performance problem around constructively.

And Furthermore…

Here are some additional mindsets to consider adopting:

- It's *LEARNING,* not *PUNISHMENT.* Again, you punish kids and criminals, not employees. Dealing with an employee's problem performance shouldn't focus on "beating them up," but instead should focus on understanding what's causing the problem and learning a way that successfully solves it and prevents it from occurring again.

- It's something you'll do **WITH** the employee, not **TO** them. It's all about working with the employee to help them find a way to solve it.

- It's something you'll do **NOW,** not **LATER.** If you don't deal with the problem as soon after it occurs as possible, you open the door for the employee to deny having any idea what you're talking about. It becomes a battle of memories, and of course it's *yours* that is faulty, not theirs...or so they'll figure. It's much more effective to be able to say, "*That.* What just happened *right there* is what I'm talking about. *That's* a problem."

  Another problem with waiting is that you open yourself up to a fairly valid criticism—if you think it's all that important, why did you wait so long to bring it up? The logical conclusion will be that you must be having a bad day, or maybe you're just using it as an excuse to unload on them. Not helpful for focusing on the problem and getting it fixed.

- You're evaluating their **PERFORMANCE,** not them as a **PERSON.** It's awfully easy for the employee to feel like you are attacking them personally and evaluating who they are. How you feel about them personally is not the issue here at all. Their not getting the work done is the issue.

  If they feel they are being personally attacked, they'll fight back all day long. On the other hand, if you can convey to them that *they're* not the problem, but rather their *work results* are, that will take away a lot of the potential for their being defensive and angry. They still aren't going to be all that happy to hear their performance is falling short, but it at least will keep you and them more focused on the problem, not on who they are.

Get Your Mind Right

Having to talk to an employee about their problem performance is seldom a picnic. It's usually uncomfortable for both the supervisor and the employee to some degree or another.

However, a huge amount of that discomfort you each feel can be taken out of the equation if you, as a supervisor, adopt the mindsets I'm suggesting and approach the employee accordingly. When you operate from those mindsets, you lessen the risk that the employee will go ballistic on you and take the whole thing as a personal attack.

When you can calmly approach the whole matter as a problem-solving exercise, where both of you are going to learn the reason for the performance problem and work out a way for it to get resolved, you'll find the employee is also calmer and will focus on the problem, not on you and why you're being such an inconsiderate, ill-informed bully.

It will take a little time and practice to break with old ways of thinking and adopt these new ways. But it will be time *very* well spent when you experience how much more smoothly the conversation goes and how it will result in noticeably better results.

14 THE CONVERSATION

At what point do you talk to an employee whose performance has dropped below expectations? As *soon* as you notice they're falling below standards and aren't producing acceptable results.

That means *now*, not later. Why's that? Well, the longer you wait:

- Memories get fuzzy—yours and theirs, so who's to say who's right and who's wrong?

- Bad work results keep piling up while you wait.

- You set yourself up for the question, "Why didn't you tell me sooner?"

- The employee may think, "It can't be all *that* bad if you were willing to wait until *now* to mention it to me."

- You may be seen as unwilling to deal with problem performance.

- Other employees may begin to wonder what you think of *their* performance, because you apparently don't always deal with problems when they happen, but later on when you feel like it.

So it's crucial to address a slump in performance as soon as it happens and find out why it's happening. It shows you're serious about employees performing at or above expectations and that you'll deal with problems as soon as they arise. If you do that consistently, you'll go a long way toward preventing future problem performers.

Whatcha Got?

You need to decide which of two scenarios you're facing—the "first-timer," or the true problem performer. What you're trying to accomplish in the conversation will be different depending on which scenario fits the employee you're going to talk to.

If you're talking to the "first-time-offender"—the employee who has *just* begun showing signs of struggling to do an acceptable job, but isn't showing a consistent pattern of not meeting expectations—your goal is to find out which of the Big Six is in play. You want to find out the reason for the poor performance so you can help them become successful as quickly as possible.

Almost always, if you really listen to a first-timer, you'll find the problem will be somewhere among the first four reasons of the Big Six. That means you'll need to do some coaching to help get them on track. You'll recall that that's the very *essence* of the supervisor's role—helping an employee be as competent as they can be.

Coaching the First-Timer

A Boss will tend to come down hard on the first-timer and tell them in no uncertain terms to get it together or else! But the employee probably isn't real clear on what to do differently. The Boss pressuring them to come up with a fix on their own—*right now*—usually only serves to ramp up the employee's frustration *and* make them anxious and resentful of the Boss. All highly motivating and helpful, don't you think?

Coaches on the other hand take a positive approach. They take the time to work *with* the employee.

Coaches will ask good questions and listen carefully to the answers. Coaches want to find out what's missing for that employee and help them fill in the gap.

So right away, *coach* an employee who is just starting to show signs of struggling and the situation will usually get resolved easily and positively. You'll develop their competency and keep them from eventually turning into a problem performer. You'll also establish your reputation as a helper, not a tyrant, which is a very *good* thing indeed for both of you!

The True Problem Performer

The true problem performer, on the other hand, isn't failing because of any of the first five reasons of the Big Six. The problem performer is squarely camped out in reason six—they just don't want to do the work. So the conversation you have with a problem performer will be very different from the one you have with a first-timer.

You won't be coaching the problem performer to make them competent at the job. They've already shown they have everything they need in order to be competent. They've shown that they *can* meet job expectations because they occasionally do so.

Instead, you'll be coaching them to decide whether to find a way to *consistently* meet job expectations, or to leave your organization.

They're not incompetent. Their problem is number six—they don't want to do the work. So the problem is entirely *theirs* to solve.

So you'll be focusing the conversation on *them* coming up with a plan for what they're going to do to fix their problem. It also means you'll make it abundantly clear that they have a *choice* to make—either create a plan for how they'll meet their job expectations from now on and follow it faithfully, or leave the organization. It's entirely their choice.

Riding the Storm

Confronting a true problem performer can sometimes get you pretty puckered up. Why's that? Well, it can stir up negative emotions in you and the employee. Employees can get defensive and argumentative. You can get frustrated and angry.

The conversation can get a bit dicey at times, but you *can* hold the uproar to a minimum.

Hanging with them through the often exasperating process of asking them good questions and listening carefully through all the excuses to find the *real* reasons can be quite a chase indeed! However, if you hang in there and stay on top of the conversation, keeping it focused on their finding their own solutions to *whatever* they say the reason is for their poor performance, they'll eventually get down to what's really going on.

From there they'll either fix their problem once and for all, or they'll move on out of the organization. Either way, the performance problem *stops*, and you no longer have to deal with the poor results you've been getting from that employee.

You can hold the uproar to a minimum if you've prepared yourself for the discussion as I described to you earlier, and you follow the step-by-step process I'll show you.

The Conversation

In a nutshell, here's what the conversation with the true problem performer is about.

The employee is failing to hold up their side of the "contract" they agreed to when they hired on. That can't continue.

The goal of this conversation is to have the employee make their choice.

They're not entitled to their job if they aren't going to do the work it requires. They can't continue to be an employee if they're not doing the work—period, end of discussion.

They need to be made aware that the choice is entirely theirs. Either they choose to get on board and do the work, or they choose not to, which means they're choosing to leave your organization.

The goal of this conversation is to have the employee make their choice.

It can be quite a challenge to have a positive, supportive and respectful conversation. However, you have to take the lead.

You need to be in control of the conversation, keeping things as calm as possible and focused on the performance issues. You can't control *their* reactions, but you can control your *own* reactions. You can control the content and direction of the conversation.

If you do that well, you can strongly influence their reactions. You can influence what they think, do and say during the conversation.

How? By structuring the conversation and sticking to that structure as the conversation progresses.

I'll describe a structure I highly recommend for doing just that. It's composed of a series of distinct steps that, if you follow them in order, will do wonders to help you remain calm and in control of the conversation.

Step By Step

It should be obvious, but I'll say it anyway—make sure you have the conversation in a private setting. *Never* have it where anyone else can see or overhear it. You owe that to the employee, their coworkers and yourself. It's a matter of protecting the employee's dignity and creating trust.

The basic steps of the conversation are:

1. Say *something* positive about their work to get things off on a good note.

2. Clearly explain to them what work results you expect.

3. Show them the evidence that they're not producing those results.

4. Get them to create their own plan for how they'll consistently produce those results.

5. Get them to commit to their plan in writing.

6. Check to see if their plan is working.

Some steps may take longer than others. However, being patient and sticking with the process will ultimately result in the performance problem getting fixed—either by the employee bringing their performance up to expectations, or deciding this job isn't for them and leaving. Either way it's fixed.

Let's look at those steps one by one.

Step 1: Start on a positive note.

There's bound to be some negativity in a conversation about problem performance. In order to try to minimize it, it's often a good idea to try to set a positive tone right off the bat. Say something positive about the employee—like things they do well, times they can be a pleasure to have on board, successes they've had.

Sure, the topic is poor performance, but the goal isn't to beat anybody up.

You may say something like, "Joe, there are lots of times where I've been able to count on you to get something done, or to pitch in and help someone out when we're in a pinch. I really appreciate it when you do those things." Or, "You have a lot to offer in this job. You've got the knowledge and skills to do almost anything around here that needs to be done."

Sure, the topic is poor performance, but the goal isn't to beat anybody up. It's to try to have the employee find a constructive solution to their problem.

It may be hard to think of something positive to say. You may be frustrated and angry with the employee for not getting the work done. You may be under pressure from your management to get the situation fixed pronto.

But there *has* to be something redeeming about this employee—the times where they *have* done a good job, some valuable skills they have, etc.

You want to set the stage for a constructive conversation and not have *everything* about it be negative. The employee needs to know that you're not against them—that you value them as an employee and want to see them successfully producing acceptable results.

If you can't come up with anything positive to say, you probably need to wait until you've gotten your attitude together…there's *got* to be something positive you can say about this employee!

Oh, and *do* sound sincere. They'll know right away if you mean what you're saying or not.

Step 2: Explain the performance expectations.

This whole conversation is anchored on the WHAT. It all comes from them not producing what you expect them to produce. As their supervisor it's your job to clearly explain what results you expect the employee to produce. It's their job to produce them.

You've got to be sure you know what results you're expecting, but you also have to be sure the *employee* understands exactly what results you're talking about here. A good way to do that is to simply ask the employee what results they understand you want. If they've got it right, go on to Step 3.

The only thing you want in this step is confirmation that they understand the work results you're asking for.

But if they aren't accurately telling you the results you're expecting, you'll have to put your communications skills to work.

You'll need to keep explaining what results you're talking about and asking them what they're hearing until they get it right.

At this point, they may sense that it's not likely going to be all grins and giggles here. So they may immediately try to short-circuit the conversation by interrupting you and putting up some defensive smoke screens. They may say things like the results you're asking for now aren't what you said they were before, or that other supervisors say something different, or that they *are* doing what you want. etc.

They're trying to deflect the "heat." If they try to take the conversation off on tangents like these, you need to bring it back and keep it focused on the work results you expect. Simply say something to them like, "We'll get into all that in a minute. Right now, I just want to make sure you fully understand exactly what results I'm expecting you to produce before we go any further here."

The only thing you want in this step is confirmation that they understand the work results you're talking about. Don't go on to the next step until they can accurately tell you what results you're expecting.

Step 3: Show them the work results that are not up to expectations.

If the employee hasn't gotten defensive yet, you can pretty much count on it happening when you get into this step. So be ready to keep things calm and focused on work results.

You see, when an employee *feels* they're being accused of doing something wrong (as they undoubtedly will when you confront them), their defense mechanisms will kick right in. They'll *immediately* start trying to redirect the conversation and deflect the trouble they see coming—*just like they did when they were* kids. (Remember that from the previous chapter?)

They'll look for any way they can to show you you're wrong in your "accusations." They didn't do it, you're wrong, their performance is nowhere near as bad as you say it is, you

> *It's absolutely **critical** that you have solid, documented evidence that they are not producing what you expect them to.*

can't prove it, they're doing exactly what you told them to, etc…etc….etc.

It's absolutely *critical* that you have solid, documented evidence that they're not producing what you expect them to. You've got to be able to say something like, "Here on this page you see what results you should be producing, and over here on *this* page you see what you've been producing. See how they're different?"

Or, "Here's a record of your work results over the past two weeks. See how they don't match the expectations we just talked about?"

You don't have a leg to stand on if you can't show them undeniable, factual, observable, measurable performance *data*.

Without hard evidence, they'll almost always argue with you about their results. If all you have are your own "observations," you'll lose the argument.

So for example, if you say, "You're always late!" they'll say "I'm never late. I'm always on time but you just don't see me." Or, "Oh yeah? I am not *always* late. I was actually in here fifteen minutes *early* yesterday!" It's just your word against theirs if you don't have documentation—*proof*, if you will.

Instead you need to be able to say, "Here is your time-clock record. See how you were late every day but one each of the last four weeks?" There's no argument. Those are the facts, plain and simple.

If you say, "You've got to pick it up here! You're behind in your production," they'll say something like, "What are you talking about? Just look at that pile of parts I've done!"

Or they may say, "Man, I really don't know what you're talking about. I'm working my butt off and I'm producing more than anybody else around here!"

But if you say instead, "Here are the daily production goals for you for the past three weeks. And here is the record of what you have produced over those same three weeks. See the number of days where your production fell short of the goal? That's eighty percent of the time." Again, nothing to argue about. You are showing them undeniable facts, not opinion.

If the employee launches into a series of excuses, you simply say to them, "We'll get into reasons why your work results don't meet expectations in a minute. For right now, I just want to make sure you understand that your results don't meet those expectations."

Once they acknowledge that gap, you can proceed on to the next step. Until they do, keep showing them the proof.

Step 4: Ask the employee to explain the performance gap.

Fasten your seatbelt—here we go!

The good news is that you're letting them *finally* get into all the reasons why they aren't getting the work results you're asking for.

The bad news is, you have to be patient (sometimes *very* patient!) while you wade through a sea of *excuses* to get to the actual *reason* they aren't performing to standards.

The employee will very likely launch into a full arsenal of excuses for why they just can't produce what you're asking them to, or why it's not *their* fault, or why this is all so unfair, etc. You can feel stonewalled at every turn as they keep coming up with one excuse after another why the problem just isn't solvable.

You need to be good at reflecting back what you're hearing.

Here's where strong active listening skills are really important. You need to be good at reflecting back what you're hearing. "So, the reason you aren't producing acceptable results is XYZ, am I hearing that right?"

If the reason they're giving you sounds weak or stupid to *them* when you repeat it back, they'll most likely change their story and come up with a different reason. To which you would again reply, "So you're telling me the reason you aren't producing acceptable results is actually ABC. Is *that* right?"

This little dance will continue until they say, "Yep, that's the reason all right!" Before you simply go with that answer, though, you've got to be listening carefully. Does what you're hearing sound at all reasonable to you?

They may be blowing a smoke screen your way. If it doesn't sound sensible, it probably isn't, so tell them so. Keep on questioning them until they come up with the real reason.

You can also say something like, "I'm not sure I understand how that's keeping you from getting acceptable results. Would you explain that a little more to me?"

This may take a while, but what you'll find is that eventually the employee will realize you're not buying any weak or phony excuses and they'll get down to the real reason. Keep asking questions and reflecting back what you're hearing. Be calm, patient, and *persistent*.

A great beauty of all this is that the employee will *eventually* tell you why they aren't doing the job. You don't have to guess at the reason. You're not making assumptions or being accusatory. You may have your suspicions, but why wonder? The truth is right before you, directly from the source. You aren't *guessing*—they're *telling* you.

Step 5: Ask them to make a plan to fix their performance problem

Now that the real reason has been identified, it's time to start asking them to come up with a plan for how they'll fix it. "Well then, if that's what's holding you back, what can you do to fix it so you *can* produce acceptable results?"

*Your expectation is clear that you expect **them to solve their own problem.***

A key concept here is that you are asking them what *they* can do that will fix the situation. Your expectation is clear that you expect *them to solve their own problem.*

Tell them you're expecting a plan that they're one-hundred percent positive will fix the problem once and for all.

This is Coaching in spades. Remember, a Coach is responsible for telling an employee what the expected work results are—the WHAT—followed by expecting the employee to think about the HOW.

In the case of a problem performer, you're holding them completely accountable for coming up with HOW they'll fix their problem and consistently produce the results you're asking for—the WHAT.

Since the problem is entirely within the problem performer's control (reason number 6), the responsibility for coming up with the HOW is entirely theirs.

Now here's the real kicker—have them write down their plan (or you write it down) in detail and *have them sign it*. Make sure it's clear in writing that this is their plan and that they are agreeing to follow that plan to fix the problem.

You'll want to pass this one by HR, but in my experience with other HR people (and my own as a former HR manager) this is a very desirable thing to do. It clearly documents *in writing* that you and the employee had a conversation about their poor performance, developed a plan to fix it that's their *own* plan, and that they agreed to follow that plan.

This written, signed plan greatly increases their commitment to following through on improving their performance—much more than just a verbal agreement. It also provides the type of documentation HR loves to have in hand should the employee fail again to improve their performance and actions need to be taken to terminate their employment.

Some words of caution here:

1. ***Don't let them get away with "I'm just going to have to try harder." Or, "I'll just have to do my best."*** This is not a level-of-effort deal. It's a matter of them coming up with a concrete plan for what they are actually, physically going to DO that will *fix* their

problem. *Now* is the time to talk about *behaviors*. A good intent is not a behavior.

You may have to say to them a number of times, "I appreciate that you're going to try harder. That's good. What I need to know is, what does "trying harder" look like? What are you actually going to physically DO that means trying 'harder'?"

2. ***Don't suggest a solution FOR them.*** If you do, they'll very likely find all kinds of reasons why it won't work. It's too hard, it doesn't really fix anything, it doesn't take into account other problems, they've tried it a million times, etc.

But if you make *them* come up with a solution, they certainly aren't going to come up with something they think is stupid, or can't do, or that they tried before, or that doesn't really fit their situation. That would be dumb and they know it.

3. ***Make it very clear that they are making the choice to stay or go.*** *They* have to solve their own problem here. They're admitting what the problem is, and only they can come up with the best way to fix it.

You need to let them know that, if they can't (or won't) solve their problem, they can't continue to be employed by your organization—plain and simple. It's their choice whether they stay or go.

So say something to them like, "You're telling me you will do ABC to get your results up to where they need to be? Can you do that? Are you one hundred percent sure that will work? Because it's going to have to if you want to continue on with us."

That will give them pause. If there is any hesitancy at all, such as "Well I *think* so," or, "Yeah I *should* be able to do it," then you respond with, "You don't sound so sure. I need a plan from you that you can *guarantee* you can do and that will fix the problem once and for all. So what would be something you *can* guarantee will work?"

And now they'll come up with a different plan. "Well, maybe I could..."

This conversation may loop around a few times as they go through all the excuses and plans they can think of. Be patient. They'll eventually know they're "cornered" and will come up with a plan you both think is reasonable and doable. That may take a little time, but it is absolutely time well spent!

4. ***Don't get sucked into being their solution.*** "Well one thing that would really help would be if you could just remind me to..." Or, "If you could get my work orders organized for me before I get in to work, then..."

You've already established that the reason they're not getting the job done isn't in the first five of the Big Six. Therefore you don't have a role to play in fixing their problem.

It is reason number 6—they just don't want to do the work. That is completely *their* problem to solve, not yours. So you may need to keep reminding them that it's up to them to fix their own problem here. They don't have to *want* to do the work—but they do have to *do* it if they want to stay!

Step 6: Follow Up

Whatever the employee's plan is, it must be implemented at the soonest opportunity. It's a "from this minute on" kind of deal. The problem needs to stop NOW and never happen again.

There also needs to be a clear understanding between you and the employee that you'll be checking their performance. Tell them when and how you're going to do that. You want to be sure the problem's been fixed. The employee needs to know what you'll be

They need to know that if they don't follow through on their plan and fix their problem, they are, in fact, telling you they're choosing to leave your organization—choice made.

looking at as proof that the problem has been fixed permanently.

If it's a tardiness issue, you'll be checking first thing tomorrow to see if they're on time. And you'll be looking at attendance data for the week, the month, etc. to ensure the tardiness has stopped.

If it's a production issue, you might be checking daily initially and then weekly or so to see that they're producing at the expected rate.

They need to know that if they don't follow through on their plan and fix their problem, they are, in fact, telling you they're choosing to leave your organization—choice made.

Review Time

So, here is a quick checklist summarizing the steps for conducting an effective conversation with the true problem performer:

- o   Prepare well for the conversation.

- o   Start on a positive note.

- o Explain what they should be producing.

- o Show them what they're producing instead.

- o Make them come up with a plan to close that gap.

- o Make sure they understand that *they* are making a choice to either do the work and stay, or not do the work and leave.

- o Write the plan down and have them sign it.

- o Follow up to ensure they're following their plan and that it's working.

Do these things well, and you'll find handling a problem performer much easier and less stressful. And you should find you get a successful solution to the problem—either the employee starts consistently producing the desired work results, or the employee leaves. Either way the problem performance has stopped!

How about some examples of how the conversation might look?

15 FOR EXAMPLE...

I've shown you a step-by-step approach for conducting a conversation with a problem performer. Let's take a look at how that might actually look in practice.

I'm going to give you three example conversations with problem employees. These are fictitious, of course, but hopefully you'll get a sense for how to structure a conversation using the step-by-step approach. Hopefully you'll also get an idea for ways to handle some of the more typical responses employees sometimes come up with in conversations like these.

Example One: Dewey

The conversation with Dewey is an example of how you would like to have most problem performer conversations turn out—expectations get clarified, a plan is created, and hopefully the problem performance gets fixed.

Dewey has been working on a production assembly line for about six months. He's one of several employees who all do the same job on that line. He receives partially completed units from the work station ahead of him and installs three additional parts to each unit before passing it on to the next work station down the line.

If Dewey hasn't installed the three parts on a unit correctly, a quality inspector removes the unit, records information about the unit on a special production report form, and places the unit into a Defect Bin. Another employee then takes the bad units out of the bin, removes the three parts from each unit and returns it all to inventory. This slows down production, and costs time and money.

The employees on that line are each expected to complete at least 125 units per week and assemble all of the units correctly the first time.

For the past four weeks here is what the Production Report shows Dewey produced:

Week 1: 90 units assembled correctly, plus 25 defective units

Week 2: 85 units assembled correctly, plus 14 defective units

Week 3: 130 units assembled correctly, plus 0 defective units

Week 4: 60 units assembled correctly, plus 38 defective units

Obviously Dewey isn't meeting production expectations. None of his coworkers are having any trouble meeting the production goals of at least 125 units per week with 0 defective units.

It's time for his supervisor (**S**) to have a chat with Dewey (**D**).

S: Hey, Dewey, can I have a minute or two to talk with you?

D: Yeah, I guess, but shouldn't it wait until I'm done working on my units?

S: I appreciate your dedication, and you can get back to it shortly. Right now it's more important that we have a little chat before you get back to work. Let's head into my office.

D: Okay.

S: Dewey, when you do good work you do very good work and I really appreciate that. But I need to have you doing very good work *all* the time.

What do you understand your production goals to be?

D: Well, I *think* you said at least 125 units per week and no defective units, right?

S: Yeah, those are the goals all right.

D: But I gotta tell you, I think they're pretty unreasonable.

S: I hear that's what you think, but nonetheless those are the goals for everybody working this line and they're not negotiable.

I've talked to you a couple of times in the past couple of months about you not always meeting your weekly production goals.

D: Yeah and I've been really trying hard to meet them.

S: Well, each time we talked you promised me you'd get your production up, but I've got your production numbers here for the past four weeks (you show him the Production Report) and you can see that you're still not consistently meeting your goals. In fact, you only met your goals one out of the past four weeks.

This is serious. This really has to stop now. I want you to fix this issue once and for all. You need to get your production numbers up starting today and keep them up from now on if you want to continue working here. I'd like to see you continue on working with us, but if you don't get your numbers up, and keep them up, you'll have to leave us.

Why aren't you hitting your goals every week?

D: Beats me. I'm doing the best I can here. Those aren't easy goals to hit.

S: The report shows you were able to hit them in Week 3. In fact you actually exceeded them that week. What was different about that week from the other three weeks?

D: Well, that week every unit I got from the other line came to me in perfect shape and I didn't have to mess around with any of them to get my parts installed on them right.

S: Dewey, QA passes every unit before it comes to you, so the units coming to you aren't ever defective. They're always the same. So that can't be the reason you didn't meet your goals the other three weeks.

Why didn't you meet your goals those three weeks, really?

D: I guess some weeks it just doesn't seem like I have enough time to get everything done.

S: Why's that?

D: I don't know. Things just happen that take up my time.

S: Like what?

D: Well, sometimes I have to go help Bob out with his units. Other times, Alice gets a big gab on and just won't quit yakking at me. Then there's times where I see things going screwy on other lines and I go see what I can do to help them out.

S: Dewey, those all seem like things that aren't really part of *your* job responsibilities. If those are keeping you from doing your own work well, what do you think you could do to make sure each of those don't get in the way of you doing *your* work?

D: Well, I guess I could tell Bob tough luck, he's on his own.

S: Yeah, but what could you say to him that might be a little more helpful for him?

D: I guess I could tell him to maybe come to you for help?

S: Do you think that would solve your problem with Bob?

D: Yeah, I suppose so.

S: Is that something you can do from now on?

D: Well, it will probably honk Bob off pretty good, but yeah, I can do that.

S: Good, sounds like you've got a plan that will take care of that. Now, what about Alice?

D: Man, now *there's* a piece of work for sure! I never met anybody who could talk that much about absolutely nothing!

S: So what can you do to keep her from distracting you and taking time away from you doing your work?

D: Hey, I've told her to shut up a bunch of times, but she just keeps on yapping at me.

S: So that doesn't seem to have worked. What could you do instead?

D: I guess I could just ignore her and keep doing my work instead of stopping to listen to her.

S: Do you think that will stop her from talking to you?

D: Probably not. She'll probably just talk louder to me. I guess I could try telling her that I can't listen to her right now 'cuz I got work to get done and maybe we could talk later?

S: Sounds like that might work. Is that something you're willing and able to do?

D: Yeah, I'll do that.

S: Sounds like another plan. Now what about those other lines having trouble? Are they part of your job responsibilities?

D: Well, not technically, but you always say how you want us all working as a team around here.

S: That's right, I do like to see you all working as a team, but I mean on your *own* line, not lines that are separate from yours.

D: Oh, I just wanted to be helpful I guess.

S: I really appreciate that, Dewey. But their work isn't part of your job. You have to let the other lines deal with their own issues unless those are creating issues for you. If that happens, please just let me know and I'll take it from there. Can you do that instead?

D: Yeah, sure, if that's what you want.

S: So here's what you've come up with if I'm hearing you correctly. Your problem meeting you're weekly goals is due to time interruptions helping Bob, stopping to listen to

Alice and going over to other lines to help them out. Do I have that right?

D: Yup, that's it.

S: And you're going to do three things to fix those problems: One, you're going to stop helping Bob out with his work and instead suggest he come to me if he needs help. Two, you're going to tell Alice you don't have time to talk because you have work to do, but maybe you can chat with her at some other time. Three, you're going to let other lines tend to their own issues and let me know if those issues are causing you problems in doing *your* job correctly.

Do I have those three plans right?

D: Yup.

S: Okay. Good job. Things are at a serious point for you now, Dewey. You have to start, and continue meeting your production goals every week. If you don't, you need to understand that you're basically choosing to leave the company.

So, let me ask you again if you believe those three plans you've come up with are going to guarantee you'll meet your goals every week?

D: Yeah. "guarantee" is a might big word, but yeah, they'll work.

S: And you're telling me that your production numbers are going to be good every week from now on?

D: Yup.

S: Okay. I'll be checking your production every day for a while, starting tomorrow, to see if you're following your plan which you say will fix the problem once and for all.

If you follow your plan, then you'll hit your numbers every week from now on. But if you aren't following your plan, then you're numbers aren't going to be there and you're basically telling me you've made the choice to leave us. And that will be final.

Do you still believe your plan will work?

D: Yeah.

S: Okay. I'm going to write your plan down and have you sign it, saying that this is *your* plan for getting your weekly numbers consistently up to goals, and that you're going to follow this plan from now on.

D: Okay.

S: Good. Thanks for working this out with me, Dewey. I want to see you be able to stay with us. Sounds like you're now going to meet your goals and, hopefully, continue to work this job for however long you'd like. The choice is all yours—choose to meet your work goals every week and you're choosing to stay with us. But remember, if your numbers fall again, you are actually telling me you've chosen to leave.

What the Supervisor Did

Let's look at that conversation with Dewey and see how the supervisor followed the steps I recommended for conducting this discussion.

FOR EXAMPLE...

The supervisor:

1. Began the conversation with something positive. *("... when you do good work you do very good work and I really appreciate that.")*

2. Made sure Dewey was clear on his performance goals—the WHAT. (*"What do you understand your production goals to be?"*)

3. Made sure Dewey knew what his actual performance was compared to those goals. (*"I've got your production numbers here for the past four weeks (you show him the Production Report) and you can see that you're still not consistently meeting your goals. You only met your goals one out of the past four weeks."*)

4. Made sure Dewey knew his unacceptable performance had reached a serious point. (*"This is serious. This really has to stop now. I want you to fix this issue once and for all."*)

5. Asked Dewey why he wasn't hitting his performance goals. (*"Why aren't you hitting your goals every week?)*

6. Pointed out Dewey was fully capable of hitting his goals, so there is no problem with the HOW. (*"The report shows you were able to hit them in Week 3."*)

7. Countered Dewey's excuse that he wasn't getting the RESOURCES he needed. (*"Dewey, QA passes every unit before it comes to you..."*)

8. Continued to press Dewey to explain why he isn't meeting his numbers. (*"Why's that?" "Like what?"*)

9. Pointed out that the things Dewey said were getting in his way weren't part of his job—the WHAT again. (*"Dewey, those all seem like things that aren't really part of your job responsibilities."*)

10. Asked Dewey what he could do to solve his problem. (*"If those are keeping you from doing your own work well, what do you think you could do to make sure each of those doesn't get in the way of you doing your work?"*)

11. Kept asking for a plan from Dewey to address each reason he gave until he came up with one they both believed would work and that Dewey would follow through on. (*"Do you think that would solve your problem with Bob?" "Is that something you can do from now on?"*)

12. Summarized the plan. (*"And you're going to do three things to fix those problems..."*)

13. Laid out the choice Dewey was going to have to make, to either stay or leave, based on whether he started consistently hitting his numbers. (*"If you don't, you need to understand that you can't stay with the company and are choosing to move on."*)

14. Put Dewey's plan in writing and had him sign it.

15. Told Dewey what the follow up would be. (*"I'm going to be checking your work each day this week to see if you're following your plan and it's working."*)

There are a few general notes about this conversation I'd like to point out:

- The supervisor had to clarify the expected work results a time or two, and let Dewey know that they weren't

- optional. Always the WHAT—it's so important that it's clear.

- It was clear Dewey was actually able (the HOW) to do the job correctly, so it isn't a competency issue requiring some coaching.

- Dewey didn't get away with blaming the product he got from the previous work station (RESOURCES).

- The supervisor didn't let Dewey get away with proposing invalid reasons, or impractical or sarcastic solutions.

This conversation resulted in Dewey coming up with his own plan for solving his production problem, and in all likelihood he now knows that it's serious that he follow through with it or else he's out the door by his own choice.

Example Two: Fern

In this next example, you'll see a different outcome for the conversation than the previous example. Here the performance problem stops, but this time it's because the employee chooses to leave the organization. That may mean some hassle for the organization to hire a replacement, but in the long run that is a better outcome for the organization than continuing to have dissatisfied customers who stop shopping there.

Fern is one of four Customer Service Reps at a retail-grocery superstore's customer service desk.

The desk is a busy place. There are often customers standing in line at the desk, while other customers are calling on the phone.

Each of the customer service reps is expected to keep customer wait time down to no more than three minutes, whether waiting in line or on the phone. Reps are also expected to make sure customers feel they're being treated politely and with respect. Ninety percent of the customers should be satisfied with how their issues were resolved.

To evaluate service rep performance, their supervisor observes the customer service desk randomly throughout the day. Each rep is timed for how long customers wait in line, or on the phone. The supervisor takes notes on how each rep interacts with customers. The percentage of customer complaints the supervisor gets on customer feedback forms and from customer phone calls is recorded daily.

There are obviously situations where a customer is being unreasonable and can't get what they're asking for. There are also times when the desk gets swamped and it just isn't possible to get to a customer within 3 minutes, but both situations are really pretty rare.

Three of the four reps are having very little trouble meeting or beating the three-minute wait time, and their customers are almost always satisfied with how their rep treated them.

Fern, on the other hand, is not doing as well. Here are the supervisor's observations of her work results for five consecutive work days:

Monday:
> Average wait time for Fern's customers: 5 minutes.
> Complaints: 40 % of her customers

Tuesday:
> Average wait time: 4 minutes
> Complaints: 30%

Wednesday:
> Average wait time: 2 minutes, 40 seconds
> Complaints: 1%

Thursday:
> Average wait time: 5 minutes 30 seconds
> Complaints: 42%

Friday:
> Average wait time: 2 minutes
> Complaints: 55%

Fern met the wait time goal only two out of five days (40% of the time), and with the exception of one day, less than 70 % (and as low as 45%) of her customers were satisfied with her handling of their issues.

THE SAVVY SUPERVISOR

It's time for the supervisor (S) to talk to Fern (F) about her job performance.

S: Fern, let's let the others handle the desk for a bit. I'd like to talk with you privately for a few minutes. Let's head to my office.

F: You sure now's a good time? I mean, things are probably going to get real busy here in a few minutes.

S: I think we'll be okay. It's important that we chat right now while the lines are short.

F: Okay, I guess.

S: Fern, what do you understand your goals are for customer wait time?

F: Well, *you* say three minutes or less, but I say...

S: Good—that's what I expect all right. And what do I expect your customer satisfaction ratings to be?

F: Something like ninety percent at least?

S: That's right.

F: But there's lots of times when...

S: Hold on just a sec. We'll get into all that in a minute. Right now I just want to make sure you know what I'm expecting from you and all the other reps.

F: Yeah, I hear you. I know that's what you think we can do every day.

S: Good.

Fern, you've shown me you're capable of doing some pretty good work at the desk. There are times when your customers have to wait only 3 minutes or less on the average, and you've been able on occasion to satisfy just about every customer you've had that day.

I'm getting concerned lately, though, because your numbers are not consistently good. For example, here are your average wait times and customer satisfaction percentages for last week (you show her the numbers).

F: Wow, you're keeping book on me? What about the other reps? They're not perfect either you know!

S: Well, yes—I *do* keep track of how all the reps are doing their jobs. Our store's business is really competitive, and if we don't do everything we can to keep our customers happy, they'll take their business elsewhere. We can't afford to let that happen.

If I don't keep track of what you reps are doing, I have no way of knowing who's doing well and who's struggling and may need my help. I track these numbers for each rep so I can make sure you're all able to meet customer service goals and doing what you can to keep customers coming back to our store.

F: Sure sounds to me like you just don't trust us.

S: It's not a matter of trust at all, Fern. It's a matter of making sure you're able to do your job well. It's my job to see that you're able to do your job and meet the performance goals we just talked about.

Now, getting back to those numbers, you can see that you only made the waiting time goal two out of five days. That's only forty percent of the time.

You can also see that you only hit the customer satisfaction percentage goal for one day last week. That was Wednesday, and in fact you pleased ninety-nine percent of them that day, which is *superb*. But the rest of the days last week you got *very* low percentages—less than fifty percent on Friday for example.

Do you have any questions about your numbers that I'm showing you?

F: No, I guess not. They don't seem right to me somehow, but you seem to have the numbers. Of course, that's only one week.

S: I can pull up the numbers for all of last month if you want me to, but they consistently follow this same basic pattern.

F: Okay, I get it.

S: Good. So what I need to know is why you can meet your goals nicely some days, but not for a lot of others.

F: Well, I just don't think it's fair for you to ask us to hit those numbers. Customers can be real fussy and impatient. They practically want us to give away the store. They think they can tell us how to do our business. I think it's a crock and impossible for any of us to do what you want us to.

S: I hear you think the goals are unreasonable. But I have to tell you that you are the only one of the four customer reps who isn't consistently hitting the goals. So that, plus the fact you *do* hit the goals sometimes, tells me that the goals really *are* reasonable and that it's possible for you to hit them.

So, why aren't you hitting them every day?

F: Well, if I try to make the customer happy it takes a long time to do that, and there goes the waiting time all shot to pieces!

S: Fern, I watched you work every day last week, and during the time I was observing you, there were at least a half dozen times just when I was watching that a customer was waiting and you weren't already working with a customer.

You were talking with that sales clerk you're friends with, Roy I think his name is. Or you were folding merchandise that had been returned. Or you were just looking at something on the desk. I couldn't tell what it was at the time.

So I don't think the problem is that you're spending too much time with other customers.

F: All right! I'll tell you what the problem is here! I'm sick and tired of these customers bellyaching to us all the time and always wanting something for nothing, or telling us how to do our job. They're a bunch of prima donnas is what they are. They think they get to have whatever they want and can order us around like we're their own personal servants.

I don't know what it is with people these days, but everybody thinks they're the *only* person in the store and that they get to have whatever they want, whether it's fair to the rest of us or not.

I've had it up to *here* with the whole lot of them and can't stand the thought of listening to one more whining crybaby coming to my desk! They're all complete idiots!

S: Fern, it sounds like you're really frustrated and angry. Sounds like you may have reached the limit of your ability to tolerate this job. Is there any way you can see your way through how you're feeling so you can hit your numbers every day from now on?

Because, when we both know you've been *able* to in the past, it's clear when you don't that you're choosing not to. You need to know that when you don't hit your numbers, you're basically making a choice to leave us and stop working here. You can't stay here if you don't hit those numbers every day.

F: Well, all I can do is try harder.

S: I appreciate that you know you'll have to put some effort into it. But effort alone isn't going to do it. What will you do to keep your emotions under control, keep wait times to three minutes or less, and leave ninety percent of your customers satisfied with your service to them?

F: I don't know, I really just don't know what I can do. Honestly, I just don't think I can take it anymore.

S: Are you saying you're giving up on it. You don't want to try anymore?

F: Truthfully, I think it is. I haven't wanted to face up to it, but I really have had it up to here with this job. I really, really need a change.

S: All right, Fern. I appreciate your honesty a lot. It sounds like you don't see a way to keep at it here. Is it maybe time for you to move on to work somewhere else where you might be happier with your work?

F: Yeah, I think it is. This job was okay at first, but it's gotten to a point now where I can't stand it. I just don't want to do it anymore. It's time for me to find something else.

S: Yeah, you know, life's too short to spend time trying to do work that just isn't us. This seems like it might be a good opportunity for you to start anew and find work you'll enjoy.

So, time to move on?

F: Yeah, it really is.

S: Okay. I'll give HR a quick call to tell them about our discussion and what you've decided. You can head right down there now and they'll help you make a smooth transition out of here.

Thank you again for being so straight with me, Fern. I'm sorry it hasn't worked out better for you here. I wish you all the best in whatever you do next. I've enjoyed knowing you! Take care and good luck!

About This Conversation

As was the case with Dewey, the supervisor followed the recommended steps for structuring the conversation with Fern.

Here are some notes about *this* example:

- The supervisor didn't let Fern get away with trying to launch into her excuses before the expected results had been clarified first.

- The supervisor nicely countered the *"you're keeping book on me"* complaint that employees sometimes use. Of *course* that's what the supervisor is doing! It's their job.

- The supervisor also nicely kept the conversation focused on *Fern's* performance and shut down her attempt to turn the conversation into a discussion about the other employees instead.

- The supervisor had direct observations of Fern on the job that disproved her claim that she was too busy to get to a customer in time. Very useful data to have, indeed!

- The supervisor didn't get sucked into Fern's emotional outbursts, or arguing with her about the specific claims she was making. Instead, the supervisor kept calm and used good active listening skills to keep the conversation focused, saying it sounded like Fern was at her limit.

- Fern wasn't allowed to get away with playing the *"I'll try harder"* card. This isn't about *effort*, it's about *actions* and *results*.

This is an example of a supervisor continuing to ask questions, stating the expectations for an employee, and pressing for actual reasons for the poor performance until the employee has to admit to the supervisor (and maybe even to herself) that this job isn't really for her anymore, and that it's time to move on.

Example Three: Claude

This third example shows how to handle the antics employees sometimes display during the course of the conversation. The trick for a supervisor is to stay calm, not get sucked into being emotional in response to the employee, and keep things focused on the employee's job performance and how they intend to fix it.

Claude works in accounting for a medium-sized organization in the aerospace industry. A major part of Claude's job is collecting financial data from various departments and projects within the company on a monthly basis and summarizing it all using a company-mandated report format.

Management relies heavily on these reports to forecast workloads, track project costs, and schedule resources efficiently. The reports are due to Claude's supervisor no later than the third Wednesday of each month.

Here is what his supervisor has recorded for Claude's reports for the past 5 months:

Month 1:   3 days late

Month 2:   1 day early

Month 3:   5 days late

Month 4:   On time

Month 5:   2 days late

Claude has turned in his report on-time only two out of the last five months. Time to have the talk.

S: Hi, Claude. Before you head back to your desk, would you come on into my office for a few minutes? I have something to talk over with you.

C: What? What do you want to talk to me about? Do we have to do it right now?

S: Well, yes I do want to talk right now, and if you'll just come on into my office I'll explain to you what it's about.

C: All right, but I hope this isn't going to take too long. I was just going to take my morning break and we don't get much time for that.

S: Hopefully this won't take too long. (Closes door).

Claude, for the most part you're doing a pretty good job for us and I appreciate the accuracy and completeness of your work. But you need to fix one area of your job—getting your monthly reports to me on time. What do you understand to be the due date for those reports?

C: Well, I'm supposed to try to get them to you around the middle of the third week or so each month if I can.

S: Close, but actually the due date is the third Wednesday of the month, and the goal isn't to just *try* to get the report turned into me by then but to actually *have* it to me by then. There's no wiggle room around that due date.

C: Well, I know that's what you'd like, but it's really hard to do that every month.

S: Every month you were late turning in that report I told you it had to be on time next time, and you promised me it *would* be. But, looking at your record for the past five months, it's obvious you're still having trouble hitting the due date. Here's the record (shows Claude the numbers). You can see that you only hit the due date two out of the past five months.

That's *not* acceptable. I need that report to me on time *every* month from now on, no exceptions.

C: That's crazy! It's not reasonable! It isn't possible most weeks. You have to cut me some slack here. Those reports take a lot of work. Nobody is hitting those dates. Why are you singling me out here?

S: Claude, I'm not singling you out. The fact of the matter is that the other accountants all get their reports in to me on time every month, with very rare exception. *You* aren't. So that's why I'm talking to you about this.

C: Oh yeah? Well just last week Connie didn't...

S: Hold on, Claude. I'm talking to *you* about *your* problem getting reports in to me on time. I'm not going to talk to you about Connie or any of the other accountants. This is about you and your performance.

Now, I see that it isn't *really* impossible for you to get them in on time because you *have* gotten them in on time twice in the past five months. So it's obvious that you *are able* to do it.

C: Well, I still think there's something screwy going on here. You're expecting too much from me.

S: Claude, I'm not going to argue with you about what I expect. I expect the same thing from you as I do everyone else. Those dates are not optional. If you want to continue working here, you have to hit those dates from now on, every week—not just now and then.

This has gotten to a very serious point for you. We've talked about this issue more than once before, and each time we've both agreed that you're capable of hitting the dates. In fact, each time we had one of those talks you hit the date the next month, but then didn't the month after that.

I need you to make a choice now—choose to either start getting these reports to me on time, every month, or choose to leave the company. The choice is all yours. Hit the numbers and stay with us, or fail to hit them and leave us.

C: All right, already, I'll do it! Sheesh!! I've about had it with this &*+!@#% conversation!!

S: Claude, I'm going to ask you to calm down, control your language and volume, and talk through this civilly with me. I'm not going to tolerate you shouting at me or losing your temper. Will you do that?

C: Yeah, I guess so.

S: Good! Now I want to know why it is that you don't get that report in on time every month.

C: Well, mostly what happens is I wait and wait for the departments and projects to send me their data so I can analyze it and put it into the report. Lots of times I don't get everything I need until it's too late. Especially from those Subcontracts clowns. *They're* who's making me late!

S: So you're telling me the problem is that you're not getting data from the departments and projects in time for your report?

C: Yeah, that's what I'm telling you. See, it isn't *my* fault! Go talk to *them*!

S: Well, I'm talking to *you* about it because you're the one that's accountable for getting these reports to me on time. I want to hear from you what your plan is going to be for how *you'll* get the information you need for that report so you can get it turned in to me on time with no more failures. What do you plan to *do*?

C: What? Me? Well, I guess I'll just have try harder to *do* it from now on! That's what I'll *do*!! All I can do is try!! But I can't be responsible for the %^&*@! departments and projects!

S: Again, Claude, keep your voice down, please, and watch your language. Now I appreciate that you are saying you'll do it. My question is, *how* will you do it? What are you actually, physically going to *do*?

What do you do *currently* to try to get that data from all departments and projects on time?

C: What? I don't *do* anything! How can I? I'm not in charge of what they do or don't do!

S: So are you telling me you just wait until it all comes in to you?

C: Yup, that's what I'm telling you.

S: That doesn't seem to be working for you, does it? What occurs to you as something you could do to get that data from them on time?

C: Beats me! What do you want me to do, march down there and kick some behind to get it from them!

S: Do you think that would go over well with them?

C: Well, no—they'd probably just go whining to their management as usual and drag their feet even more just to spite me!

S: So that doesn't sound like a very good plan then, does it? What else could you do that might be more effective?

C: I guess I could try giving them a schedule for when I need their data, and then send them reminder emails each month.

S: Think that would do it?

C: Well, it might.

S: You're sounding a bit unsure about it. What could you do that you think would do it for sure?

C: Well, maybe I could follow up the email with a phone call reminding them?

S: Sounds good, depending on how you handle yourself in the email and phone calls. If you come on to them in a huff and act as aggressively as you've acted a couple of times with me in this conversation, it may backfire on you.

C: Yeah, I guess it probably would. They just make me so mad, it's hard to control myself.

S: Can you think of any way to keep yourself calm?

C: Maybe if you would look at my emails first, to help me write them nicely, and help me find a calm way to approach them on the phone. That would help me not blow it.

S: Sure, I'd be happy to help you out that way. No problem.

So is that your plan then? You're going to do the timely reminder emails and make the phone calls? And you're planning to ask me to look over your emails before you send them, and rehearse your phone calls with you when you want me to, to help you practice being calm and polite?

C: Yeah, that's what I'll do.

S: Sounds good, Claude. It's *very* important that your plan works and that you get this problem fixed now, once and for all.

I'm going to ask you to put your plan into writing, sign it and give me the original copy. That way we both have documentation that we talked, that you came up with a plan you're sure will solve the problem, and that you're going to follow your plan and fix the problem.

It sounds like a good plan to me. If that gets you the data you need on time so you can get your reports in to me by the due date, problem solved.

Just remember, this is put-up or shut-up time. If you choose not to follow your plan and are late again, you'll have basically made the choice to leave the company. I hope you understand that you're the one doing the choosing here.

I know this has been hard for you to talk this through with me, but I appreciate you being able to stick with it and work out a good solution. It will be nice for both of us to have things going smoothly around these reports from now on.

Thanks, Claude!

Keeping On Task

Overall, notice how the supervisor kept the conversation focused regardless of how Claude was acting by:

- Remaining calm.

- Generally not getting sucked into arguments Claude tries to start.

- Clarifying the goal when Claude was being pretty vague about what the due date was.

- Not getting defensive when Claude said the goal was "crazy," and unreasonable.

- Not biting when Claude played the *"you're singling me out"* card.

- Making it clear to Claude that they weren't going to talk about Connie or any other employee—just about Claude.

- Calmly pointing out that it wasn't *impossible* for Claude to hit his numbers because he did so two out of the past five months.

- Refusing to argue about the performance expectations or defend them in any way.

- Asking Claude to calm himself down and control himself in this conversation.

- Ignoring Claude's attempt to blame the other departments for his problem.

- Asking Claude if he really thought it would work to go "kick some behind."

- Not allowing Claude to just say he'll just get it done, but pushing him to come up with what he'll actually *do* to get it done.
- Practicing active listening throughout the conversation.

This conversation could easily have escalated into a shouting match, with each attacking the other. As it is, the way the supervisor refused to get unnerved and kept responding to Claude in a calm, rational, firm manner kept Claude's responses fairly well-controlled. It at least kept from adding any fuel to Claude's fire.

Now It's Your Turn

Hopefully these examples have been helpful. Of course every situation is unique, but the structure I've shown you gives you a way to organize your thinking and successfully conduct the conversation regardless.

It's important for you to keep in mind that talking to an employee when they first show signs of struggling will very often prevent them from becoming a true problem performer in the first place. So pay attention to how employees are doing—especially the newer ones.

Coach employees early on. Help them succeed. Don't let them flounder until they give up and become someone you need to have one of these conversations with. It's all so much better for everyone that way!

A FINAL WORD...OR TWO

So there you have it—my guide to being a savvy, successful supervisor. The more you apply the ideas and techniques I've shown you in this book, the better this supervising thing is going to go for you and for the people you supervise.

Here's a little something to keep in mind as you go about supervising this way. If what you're doing as a result of reading this book is different from what you *have* been doing, you're probably going to notice a fairly common phenomenon.

Employees will pick up pretty quickly that *something* different is going on here. They're smart that way. They're hard to fool. You're not acting like you usually do. They'll wonder what's up.

You don't have to keep what you're doing a big secret from them. Let them know what changes you're making about how you supervise and why. Help them understand that what you're doing can actually benefit them, and *how*.

They may be a little cautious, maybe even nervous at first. They may initially sort of freeze in place and just stare at you with the deer-in-the-headlights look, trying to figure out what you're up to. Then they may start pushing back as you change things.

The strange thing here is that, even if they've been critical about how you supervise them, the fact of the matter is they are *used* to how you've been supervising them. They can pretty well predict how you're going to act, and react, in most work situations.

That ability to predict what you're going to do or say makes them comfy, even if they might not really like it. It's the "devil-you-know" thing—it's easier to tolerate what you know even if you don't like it than it is to tolerate the uncertainty of not knowing what's going on.

So, until they get to know the "new you," they're likely to be a bit nervous and hesitant. So what to do? JUST KEEP AT IT.

They'll eventually stop pushing back and get comfy again. They can once again predict you, only now they'll like what they're predicting much better. And, they'll be much happier in their job.

Be patient. Stay the course. Just keep at it and it *will* work. Once they experience how much better things are for them in their jobs, the momentum will keep going all by itself with decreasing effort on your part.

They'll be managing themselves and their work well, more and more, on their own!!

And that's the goal of this whole approach to supervising.

And so...

I really hope what I've given you here has been, and will continue to be, helpful to you. As I said early in this book, I believe supervising is the hardest and most important job in any organization—bar none. Without you supervising well, work just doesn't get done. Organizations don't survive.

A FINAL WORD...OR TWO

Organizations have mighty goals and strategies, but those just don't come into being without your supervising well. You're working on the front line with the people who physically make the products and provide the services that are the very reason for the organization's existence.

The organization picks the destination, but you and those you supervise are driving the bus to get there.

Hopefully I've convinced you that those you supervise will do a great job if you treat them like adults and help them be as competent in their jobs as they can possibly be. They're not your private army. They're you're allies. You do your job well by helping them manage *their* jobs well, and together you'll find success.

I've seen this approach work very well many times in many organizations. And, I believe it will work well for you, wherever you work and however far along you are in your supervisory career.

So have at it! I wish you all the best—it's yours for the taking!

ABOUT THE AUTHOR

For over 30 years, Bill Willging has provided consulting and training in project management, work team effectiveness, manager coaching and supervisory skills. His experience as an internal consultant includes providing leadership, consulting and training as an organization development specialist and human resources manager. His experience as an external consultant includes providing consulting and training for many large and small organizations in the public, private, for-profit and non-profit sectors. He earned his Ph.D. in Industrial/Organizational Psychology and has served as adjunct faculty for the Haworth College of Business and the School of Public Affairs and Administration at Western Michigan University, and for Davenport University.

www.ingramcontent.com/pod-product-compliance
Lightning Source LLC
Chambersburg PA
CBHW032302210326
41520CB00047B/900